A Buddhist in the Classroom

A Buddhist in the Classroom

Sid Brown

State University of New York Press

Published by State University of New York Press, Albany

© 2008 State University of New York

For information, contact State University of New York Press, Albany, NY
www.sunypress.edu

Production by Kelli LeRoux
Marketing by Anne M. Valentine

Library of Congress Cataloging-in-Publication Data
Brown, Sid, 1961–
    A Buddhist in the classroom / Sid Brown
        p.   cm.
    Includes bibliographical references and index.
    ISBN 978-0-7914-7597-3 (hardcover : alk. paper) —
    ISBN 978-0-7914-7598-0 (pbk. : alk. paper)
    1. Teaching—Religious aspects—Buddhism.
    2. Buddhism—Social aspects.
    I. Title.
    LB1027.22.B76 2009
    294.307'1—dc22   2007050722

10 9 8 7 6 5 4 3 2 1

To my mother, Nadine M. Brown,
and in loving memory of
my father, Charles A. Brown, III,
and my brother, Michael James Brown

Contents

Preface

One night as I was writing this book I joined some acquaintances for dinner. Delighted to be making new friends amid the clattering and yelling in the restaurant, I talked freely and listened with interest. Most of the stories were about our jobs—everyone at the table worked in university settings, some as faculty, some as staff, some at large state universities, some at small liberal arts colleges. Eventually one person asked me what I was doing on my sabbatical. I paused and looked down. The secrets making me feel awkward and reluctant to discuss my book were two: I wasn't writing the academic book I had originally planned to write, and I felt the more personal book I was writing left me too exposed. I hardly wanted to reveal what was paining me already in its exposure, but maybe it was time to own up to what I was spending hours alone each day doing. I gathered some courage and said I was writing a book about how Buddhist practices and stories influence my teaching.

My questioner's eyes widened. She shoved her hair behind her shoulder and leaned in, her face close to mine. I was a rabbit trapped by a snake. "Isn't that exactly what we should be trying to avoid?" she asked. "Bringing religion into the classroom?"

If bringing religion into the classroom means expecting or even desiring students to convert to a certain religion or to become religious in a certain way, I agree. My questioner is correct. That is exactly what we should try to avoid. Education is not about moralizing or coercion; it's about liberating and enabling students to work through the challenges of life, of the world.

But if one understands religion as it functions—as symbols, stories, institutions, ethics, values, and practices that make life meaningful—then any teacher of the humanities, and to a certain degree the social and natural sciences, brings his or her religion into the classroom. Through what teachers choose to include and emphasize and what we choose to exclude and de-emphasize, we display our view of the world and what we value. Further, through how we interact with students and the qualities of our relationships with them, we not only display our view of the world but also create it. As Robert A. Orsi writes, "Moral inquiry proceeds, like everything else in culture, through conversation. . . . Such inquiry never exists apart from conversations among real, historically situated people, and moral inquiry is always simultaneous with efforts to make its doubts and decisions public."[1] In classrooms, students learn all sorts of values: greed for money and status, hard work and joy in the excellence of others. They learn cynicism; they learn hope. So do we. Both students and teachers, in fact, learn all these things in the complex social situation of the classroom.

I write this book to communicate simply and directly how I have come to think about teaching. My teaching has been informed by my religious commitment and practices as well as by research on effective learning. Both influences are found in this book. From the perspective of a scholar of Buddhism and one who has been a Buddhist since 1983, having studied and conducted research in Sri Lanka, India, Japan, Thailand, as well as in the United States, readers will learn about Buddhism. They will also learn about teaching and learning from the perspective of someone who's been teaching different subjects in different circumstances to different age groups since the mid-1970s. I've taught swimming, philosophy, religion, English as a second language, and calisthenics in countries as different from each other as Thailand and the U.S. and in institutions as different as the University of Virginia, Iowa's Simpson College, and Chulalongkorn University in Thailand. Also, because I view teaching in practical as well as contemplative ways, this book includes practical tools as well as reflection. I hope teachers find it useful both in their teaching and in their thinking about teaching.

My father always said I wanted to become a professor as soon as I learned what a professor was. As much as such claims can be, this one is true. Once I had met Professor Thomas Flynn,[2] I was determined to become a teacher. He knew so much, could speak so well on such interesting subjects in class and listened so carefully and leisurely when we met in his office, surrounded by all those books and papers. I wanted to be like that: deeply immersed in an area of study with enough time and inclination to care deeply that others who wanted to could learn.

This book, then, is an invitation to teachers of all subjects at the high school and college levels to reflect on their work as I reflect on mine. I hope what I have to offer here is useful even though many readers teach in very different contexts and teach very different students. A lot of this book is about the intimacy of teaching and its implications and what Buddhist stories, rituals, and values can bring to that intimacy and how that intimacy relates to solving environmental and social problems. In any case, readers need know nothing about Buddhism or religion and certainly need no commitment to any religion in order to enjoy the book. Rather, all you need is to love an area of study and to have the time and inclination to care deeply about the learning of others.

Acknowledgments

The author thanks the following for permission to use several of the epigraphs.

The epigraphs for the introduction and for chapters 1, 5, and 8 come from *The Dhammapada: The Sayings of the Buddha*, translated by John Ross Carter and Mahinda Palihawdana, Oxford University Press, Oxford, 1987, pages 4, 9, 58, and 11, respectively. Used by permission of Oxford University Press, Inc.

The epigraphs for chapters 2, 3, and 7 come from *The Middle Length Discourses of the Buddha: A New Translation of* Majjhima Nikaya, original translation by Bhikkhu Nanamoli, translation edited and revised by Bhikkhu Bodhi, Wisdom Publications, Somerville, MA, 1995, pages 1011, 128, and 534–35, respectively.

The epigraph for chapter 4 comes from *The Connected Discourses of the Buddha: A Translation of the* Samyutta Nikaya, translated by Bhikkhu Bodhi, Wisdom Publications, Somerville, MA, 2000, page 1846.

The epigraph for chapter 6 comes from *Being Good* by Master Hsing Yun, translated by Tom Graham, published by Weatherhill, Inc., Trumball, CT, 1998, page 60.

I am grateful to countless teachers who have made the effort and taken the time to give me attention and share their wisdom, including the late Sister Ayya Khema of Parappaduwa Nun's Island in Sri Lanka, Dr. Thomas Flynn of Emory University, Dr. Roger Betsworth of Simpson College, Greg Smith of Vero Beach High School, Dr. Lawrence Cunningham now of the University of Notre Dame, Dr. Stephanie Kaza of the University of Vermont, Maechī Wabī, and Drs. Susan MacKinnon, Karen Lang, Jeffrey Hopkins, and Paul Groner of the University of Virginia. I am also grateful to Dr. Jonathan Sulkin then of Emory University and to Dr. Rhonda Venable of Vanderbilt University. Thank you to Drs. Tara Doyle and Robert Pryor for introducing me to India and Buddhism through the Antioch Education Abroad program. I have benefited from the tutelage of six professors of Naropa University: Zoe Avstreih, Richard Brown, Susan Burggraf, Barbara Dilley, Mark Miller, Judith Simmer-Brown, and from Mirabai Bush of the Center for Contemplative Mind in Society. Most recently I have learned much from Phillip Moffitt, Eugene Cash, and Sally Clough Armstrong of Spirit Rock Meditation Center and from Thanissaro Bhikkhu of Wat Mettavanaram.

I owe special thanks to my three American Academy of Religion friends who guide me in teaching: Beth Blissman of Oberlin College, Grace Burford of Prescott College, and Fran Grace of the University of Redlands.

Many of my students have helped me learn about learning. These include: Kami Bruner, Cheryl Burns, Penelope Powell, Emily Wright-Timko, Andrew Schmidt, Derek Lemoine, Whitney White, Haley Merrill, Mary Bruce Gray, Katharine Wilkinson,

Jamey Lowdermilk, Caitlin McCollister, Melissa Early, Kate S. Cummings, and Madeleine Rowe.

All the students in Buddhism and the Environment deserve my gratitude: Mattie Azurmendi, Anita Rhiannon Bond, Renee Brockinton, Mitchell E. Burdett, Jillian L. Burgess, Mary C. Carter, Robert F. Chapman, Emily H. Crowe, Sarah H. Harder, Andrew A. King, Jeanne B. Lumpkin, Shawn E. Means, Christie A. Peeler, Wade P. Reynolds, Amy E. Robertson, Maria P. Rodriguez, Taylor M. Rogers, Robin M. Rotman, Anthony J. Zucchero. Thank you for your patience, excitement, engagement, and curiosity.

I extend special thanks to Helen Benet-Goodman for her initial conversation about the importance of narrative as one reflects on teaching, leading to the chapter on Angulimala. Also to Julie Puttgen for inspiring the cover art. For more information on her Internet Mandala Project, see http://www.turtlenosedsnake.com/imp.htm.

My oldest friend, Rebecca Barnhouse, suggested the topic for this book. Would that everyone on earth had a friend capable of giving such fine guidance and able to reward effort so well.

Finally, I extend my deepest thanks to Lucia K. Dale.

In the Event of a Crash Landing

Having known the essential as the essential,
And the superficial as the superficial,
They attain the essential
Who are in the pastures of proper intentions.
—*Dhammapada* 12

In nine more minutes, I would hand out the course evaluation forms and end the semester. With a research leave and a summer ahead of me, I wouldn't teach for another eight months. Tired, wanting to put this school year behind me, I struggled to remain present in the class, to attend to what was in front of me. The students lined the walls of the classroom, facing inward and sitting in straight-backed, oak chairs with wicker seats. Tall, narrow windows with oiled oak moldings framed the quad outside.

I had invited students to talk about the class in order to bring some kind of closure to this exceedingly lively, engaged, exciting, difficult-to-contain-and-direct ("intractable" seems such a negative term) group of twenty-five students. Today their comments and questions created a smooth waltz, evidence of the practice we'd had all semester and the seriousness of our purpose.

Then one impassioned student declared loudly that we had done nothing all semester. "We shouldn't fool ourselves about our accomplishments," Jessie said.[1]

Time seemed to stop. Some students' mouths hung open. Some eyed each other surreptitiously. Others turned reflexively to me. No one wanted to break the silence, but everyone wanted that silence broken.

I raised my eyebrows in invitation for other comments and let the discussion continue.

Later I wondered at my lack of emotion. Was I so weary of this class, of teaching, that I felt nothing when faced with this sort of assessment? Or was this instead an equanimity that comes from years of practice with the emotional outbursts of twenty-year-olds? Was it shock? Did I still care?

I adore teaching. I love creating a natural learning environment and being there with students. I love trying to discern where students are in their intellectual, social, ethical, and personal development and then finding ways to create experiences, discussions, and occasions for rushes forward. By doing so I try to help them become more knowledgeable, more caring for those around them, more responsive to the challenges of our age. I treasure learning from students what makes them care for or despise something, what their dreams for our society and world are, where their pain and joys lie. I love a silent room as students ponder; I love a boisterous room as students struggle. I will never forget one student coming into my office the day after I had defined religion as making meaning.[2] She was struck by the thought that she should focus on making her life meaningful. She looked as if she'd found a shiny little key on the sidewalk and wasn't sure what it might unlock.

So what are the most important aspects of teaching for me?

While I enjoy the challenges of staying abreast of my field in order to teach well, the kind of thinking about teaching that really moves me is about learning itself. I appreciate understanding how learning takes place. As I design courses, I consider the ways fieldwork, class discussions, and readings will show in brilliant colors the limits of rigid and unbeneficial frameworks of thinking. Of course, it's not enough to show problems. I also encourage students to cherish what works for them and to articulate their values. I like to help students get what they need to build their next frameworks and act on them. A fulfilling and contributing life requires one to break down old and create new frameworks—new worlds, really—fairly often. I help my students understand that a meaningful life requires responsible and effective action. In return, they do the same for me. No matter how much I know, I always learn more from my students.

When I designed my Buddhism and the Environment class, the one on the last day of which Jessie questioned the value of everything we'd done, I did what I always do as I design a class.

I kept my university's statement of purpose in mind. It speaks of "developing the whole person through a liberal arts education of high quality" and stresses "training in personal initiative, social consciousness, aesthetic perception, intellectual curiosity and integrity."[3] In response to these ideals, I tried to ask the questions that will result in the kind of deep learning that changes outlooks and lives in those directions, questions based on those Ken Bain suggests in his *What the Best College Teachers Do*.[4] For example:

1. What do I really want students to be able to do intellectually, physically, emotionally, and socially when they've taken this course? What do I want them to be able to notice and analyze?
2. Why?
3. What experiences, readings, and activities will help them to develop in these ways?
4. How might I invite them to make the world a little better in light of who they are and what they now understand and value? (How can I call them to conscience and motivate them to respond to that call?)
5. How will I be able to tell how well the students are doing and how can I encourage them to articulate what they are learning?

In order to teach well, I also read many books on teaching, such as Bain's.[5] Further, I try to learn constantly about how the brain works. I read what I can to understand what my own brain is like and how it functions and how it compares to those of my students, who are considerably younger than I am.[6] I also pay attention to what needs—especially in terms of our environment—our world has. My students need to know that though they've never knowingly met someone with tuberculosis, it's what a lot of people die of. They need to know that tens of thousands of children die every day of starvation though there is enough food to feed them. They need to know that what and how we eat, how we transport and entertain ourselves are unsustainable—that human beings and entire ecosystems are dying to support our lifestyles. Finally, I learn more and more about what it takes to act effectively in the world. Reading about the latter helps me understand what we professors expect of and hope for our students: we not only want them to be able to think well—reflectively, abstractly, critically, creatively—but also we don't want them to rob homes. And not only do we want them to refrain from harming others, we want them to, well, do good. We want them to undermine systems that oppress, and support and strengthen the ones that help people. We want our students to help others get enough food to eat and clean water to drink, have dignity as well as meaningful work. After all, we want them to, as Robert Kegan puts it, "identify their inner motivations, acknowledge internal emotional conflict, be to some extent psychologically self-reflective, and have some capacity for insight and productive self-consciousness." In developing their minds, identifying our world's problems and working to solve those problems, we want our students to live vibrant, meaningful, helpful lives.[7]

So I bring to teaching a toolbox, and I try to reach for the right tool at the right time.[8]

One tool alone won't do. When I want to learn a poem, I read the first lines aloud, cover them, try to recite them from memory, peek, read them aloud again, try to recite them from memory. When I want to understand the relationship between the amygdala and emotions, I might take some notes and draw a diagram. When I want to learn a methodological approach, sometimes all I can do is submit to an explanation of it in awe, doing all I can to keep my attention on the text while in fact so excited that my whole body wants to jump up and do something else—it's overexcited by the theory, so overexcited that it can only enjoy and savor the feeling (and often is so overwhelming I tend to end the experience by getting a cup of tea or letting the cat out). So just as there are many different ways of learning, there are many different ways of teaching and many roots through which to draw the nutrients that lead to a blossom in the classroom. All these examples are different ways of learning, and so require different ways of teaching.

So what had I done in my Buddhism and the Environment class wherein, nine minutes before I handed out the evaluations, Jessie so harshly dismissed our semester's worth of work?

I had taken *huge* risks. Some of those risks included teaching the course in the absence of available models. I knew of only one other professor who had taught a class like it before, and she approached the subject in a wholly different way—as one might expect, since she is a biologist and I am a scholar of religion.

Another risk I took was in self-consciously organizing the class in response to practical, environmental concerns. We in the United States damage the environment most significantly by how we transport ourselves and what we eat, so I organized the class to allow students a lot of time to consider these particular problems and how Buddhists and those committed to sustainability approach them.[9] Was teaching a course in response to such practical concerns even *allowed* in academia? Was I sacrificing the respect of my peers by abandoning even the veil of objectivity as we responded to the particular environmental problems each of us in the class contributed to every day?

The greatest peril came in implementing a series of personal experiments in which students explored various core understandings and practices of both Buddhists and environmentalists.[10] In them, students tried a variety of practices for short periods of time, usually a week. The experiments allowed them time for sustained reflection on their relationship with the natural world. (Without knowing more about this relationship, how could they know how and whether they already valued it? How could they see its importance to the Buddhist thinkers we studied?) These activities also helped them develop empathy for Buddhists by inviting them to engage in Buddhist practices and ethics. They learned to develop a critical view of consumer culture when they self-consciously disengaged from that culture. Students also developed a critical view of other aspects of our culture that prevent us from living sustainably. (See later in this chapter and Appendix I for more details on the experiments.)

What entails risk, of course, differs from field to field and person to person, but the ways I tempted fate in this class became clear in retrospect. Through the structure of the class, I had forced greater personal involvement with the material, in a wider variety of ways, than I had done before. Before I taught the class, I didn't know how my students would respond, and I didn't know what the implications of those responses were for me. Further, because both religion and the environment are often emotional issues, I had exponentially increased the emotional volatility of the class just by combining these topics into one class.

Combining the topics also invited disaster because doing so brought to the public eye the aspects of my life that lie closest to my heart: Buddhism and environmentalism.

* * *

Like my student who found the little golden key, when I was in college I too thirsted for meaning. In each class, I felt my intellect develop in new and fascinating ways, but to what end? I wondered if I were only learning intellectual game-playing and if that was all I could hope for. With the duality and finality I often see now in my own students, I decided in my junior year to drop out of college to become a religious. I knew nothing of religion and had never even taken a class in the subject much less interviewed anyone who had chosen that path. But maybe by leaving college and committing myself fully to religion I would find what I was looking for.

I anticipated parental resistance. My father, in particular, was eager for another of his children to finish college. I was the last of seven children and only two had earned their degrees by then. My quitting college with only a year to go was going to hurt him.

Just as I wandered across campus mentally writing the letter of explanation to my father, I looked up and saw a poster advertising an opportunity to "earn college credit while you live in a monastery." This solved all my problems—I could find meaning without hurting my father. It was only after I'd decided to apply that I realized the poster referred to a *Buddhist* monastery in *India*.

There I meditated at least two hours a day, followed a monastic time schedule, and took the five standard precepts of the religion (to abstain from taking life, stealing, sexual misconduct, false speech, and ingesting intoxicants). Meditation study required careful reading and listening as well as attention to my own experience. Just as I later asked my students to try a practice and see its results, so did my teachers ask this of me. Daily I engaged in life-changing interior practices as well as experiential learning—all for the sake of relieving suffering, the primary goal of Buddhist practice. Grounding my own experience of the world in a tradition 2,500 years old shaved the fluff off me. It left me more honest, less self-involved, and oddly both resilient and naked. The greater resilience and naked honesty gave me a new calm and generosity. I understood better what I should do; my perceptions were clearer; I had a better idea of what I was striving for. I didn't rush to defend myself against perceived slights as often. I sought to understand and help others more.

While I lived in the monastery, I was also living in one of the poorest states in India. This meant that when, for the first time, I saw what starving to death looked like, I was forced to reflect on it instead of turning away (finding a distraction, for example, in entertainment). I met farmers living at the mercy of the weather. I saw disabled children limping along supported on rough crutches made of tree branches. I was forced to ask myself about my father, who had been physically disabled by and in constant pain from rheumatoid arthritis since I was two. What would have happened to him had he lived in Bihar, India? How about my physically disabled and mentally challenged brother? What kind of life would he have led? For how long? My reflections became very personal, indeed.

My interest in the environment bloomed right after my return to college from India, when I finally took the science course required for my liberal arts education: Introduction to Environmental Studies. The soil was fertile: my mother and maternal grandfather communicated their appreciation of natural beauty and respect for wonder through their painting. To commemorate her father's death, my mother walked the beach, picking up trash. My own involvement in the ecology club in my junior high school and its projects such as mangrove-planting taught me aspects of ecology and gave me a sense of urgency. I cultivated mangrove seeds at home and witnessed how they could prevent erosion problems increased by the construction that intensified every day in south Florida, where I lived.

The college environmental studies course left me enchanted, challenged, and finally: committed. In that class I began to get a view of global problems, and my experiences in India helped me to understand their immediacy. While my fellow students sat disbelieving and appalled as we read how many people in the world use dung as cooking fuel, I nodded my head. I'd eaten food cooked on a dung fire. I had seen a deep level of poverty and lived in an agriculturally based village. As I learned, I was confronted with a dilemma: given the systemic problems that make mainstream American lifestyles so unsustainable, so unethical, how could I live an ethical life and still live in America? When the textbook[11] suggested that many transportation, pollution, and nonrenewable energy issues would disappear if everyone in the world tried to live near where they worked and bicycled or walked for every trip under five miles, I vowed to do so. (Many

Americans accept the "necessity" of a car without question, not realizing the health and financial costs of dependence on automobiles. While it's difficult to communicate the personal health costs, the individual's financial costs are more clear: The American Automobile Association estimates the cost of using a car to be $6822 per year [based on driving 10,000 miles per year and includes gas, oil, maintenance, insurance, license]. That's 64 percent of the salary of someone working for minimum wage and 28 percent of the salary of someone getting paid four dollars more an hour than minimum wage, which brings a family of four "up" to the poverty level, according to the Department of Health and Human Services. The societal and environmental costs, of course, are large as well and even more insidious and difficult to communicate.)

Cycling this much was at least one concrete way I could help the world, and it reinforced what I had come to understand of the Buddhist principle of *paṭicca-samuppāda*, variously translated as dependent co-arising, dependent origination, interdependence, mutual causality. *Paṭicca samuppāda* basically means that "everything arises through mutual conditioning in reciprocal interaction."[12] Everything exists in a matrix of all other things, so every thing affects other things, so nothing is somehow separate or exempt from anything else. Everything affects something else.

What a difference cycling and recognizing its effects have made in my perspective: I am more connected with the outside world and more deeply understand aspects of sustainability. When it rains, I get wet. When frogs are calling from the ditches as I go by, I hear them. When I haven't eaten properly, I don't feel as energetic and I can't go as fast. Cycling also provides opportunities for the kind of physical exertion and free time that allow me to be more creative.

* * *

After I taught Buddhism and the Environment, I realized I had designed a class that reflected, and perhaps even mirrored, the experiential foundations of my interests both in Buddhism (through meditation) and the environment (through cycling). I had worked to inspire in students the self-awareness and reflection these activities inspired in me. Further, I had integrated into the course ways to reflect on the experiences and ways to examine our culpability in a society that places such stress on our natural systems. While of course the readings and class discussions were as integral to the course as studying Buddhist philosophy and environmental principles and concepts were to my understanding of those fields, I had included experiences and opportunities for reflection that forced students in the Buddhism and the Environment course to create frameworks for understanding as wide as those I had created in my own final year of college. I had also given them (through the experiments such as mine with cycling) a sense of the liberation that can come of commitment—how trying out a vow to an ethical practice can liberate one to see and respond to new things. You make the vow, and the vow makes you.

The carefully tailored experiments and sustained reflection on them became the center of the course. All students deepened and explored their connections with nature by engaging in a Plant Companionship Experience—they were required to choose one plant on campus and spend an hour with it each week.[13] Further, during the last half of the semester, students conducted four other experiments, chosen from a list of six. Most experiments lasted a week, and everyone engaged in a particular experiment did so simultaneously. The topics of the experiments paralleled what we studied. For example, when we read a high-pitched squealing book about the impact of car culture on the United States, students could avoid vehicles that relied on fossil fuels. When we read about the impact of industrial agriculture on our environment, especially of raising cows for food, students could opt to go vegetarian. When they read Buddhist critiques of consumerism, they could refrain from buying anything besides food. As we studied meditation, they could meditate or engage in contemplative prayer. (This experiment lasted three weeks.) The students engaged in each week's experiment were invited to talk about their problems, reflections, and insights on the topic in the classroom—in effect, they became experiential experts. Their responsibilities as experts helped students deepen their reflection, as did the journals all students were required to keep. I sometimes gave specific topics for students to write about; I often used class time to generate topics and discover and address journal problems.

If the papers are any indication, the class was a brilliant success. Four of the first papers were so good I suggested the students try to get them published. These papers were also read by a good friend who, as a professor of English, is understandably reluctant to read papers written by other people's students. She put them in her permanent file and will use them the next time she teaches the book the students analyzed. Most of the students wrote fascinating, careful, reflective papers they can be proud of for years to come.

But papers are just one way to assess the class. Perhaps it would be better to consider the class discussions. They were always lively, intense—sometimes even frightening. While on occasion we were glad to see the end of the class period because our discussions were so exhausting, so worrisome, sometimes even painful, we often wished for more time to continue speaking, listening, apologizing, understanding, exploring, clarifying. No wonder. We had begun the class reading a novel that explores the effects of consumerism and then read a book on Buddhist philosophy, which they used to investigate the novel.[14] Once the students had learned how to analyze using tools from Buddhist philosophy and learned how some of their daily habits affected the environment, they could begin to see how Buddhist thinkers might approach these questions. As they began to read what Buddhist thinkers had to say about the environment, their own analyses grew more skillful. These intellectual gains were deepened and spiced by personal experiences and reflections on their own ethical lives.

In the end, I know—from their written work and from our discussions both in and out of class—my students learned a lot about Buddhism and a lot about the environmental challenges we face. From the evaluations, I know they appreciated the class and the approaches I took. They were forced to consider deep questions about their own place in the world, their ethics, and their relationship to the environment. They had experiences that I think may help keep these questions at the forefront of their lives for a while. They will face their futures with more questions, more awareness of the topics we addressed and more sensitivity to some of the basic problems we face. And I hope in several years they might still be able to give a Buddhist analysis of a situation based on their learning in the class.

* * *

Yet what Jessie most wanted to express on that final day was her intense frustration with the class. How am I, who spend so much of my time deeply questioning the nature of learning and teaching, to understand her comment?

Not long after I distributed the student evaluation forms and left the room, Jessie rushed down the hall to my office. "I didn't mean what I said," she began, working to catch her breath. No, she hadn't meant what she said. As she talked, it became clear that she'd meant that the problems we had addressed in the class were huge and frightening and frustrating. She'd meant that our limiting worldviews (and those of her fellow students seemingly more so) were often entrenched, difficult to change. She'd meant that it was hard to generate attention and open-mindedness, or even see the value of doing so, in the face of arguments from people with whom we disagree. Her comment indicated that she was right about where she should be in terms of her logical-cognitive, social-cognitive, and intrapersonal-affective domains[15] but that she would have to go further in order to contribute to our larger society and face the astonishing challenges it begs us to accept. She'd meant, "But what next?"

She'd meant that she was feeling growing pains; her comment in class was a groan in response.

She'd also meant, I think, that the class had too many people in it, that I hadn't directed our conversations as well I might, that I had aroused more interest and engagement than I had fostered resolution and coherence. All true. My own fears and excitement about the course led me to make some basic errors, such as accepting ten students over the limit. (A class, after all, cannot be allowed to become larger and larger just because students ask to be admitted to it, no matter how much it seems like a party that will be more fun the more crowded the room is.) The size contributed to the problems in coherence—there were simply too many competing voices striving to be heard. Listening to Jessie's frustrations about the class helped me clarify my own. While I wanted to argue with Jessie ("It wasn't all that bad!"), I knew she was right about many things.

Later, seven hours after that class ended, seven hours and nine minutes after Jessie shocked us all with her remark, even though I knew I wouldn't be in a classroom for eight solid months, I found myself on my living room couch, a pile of books about teaching on my lap, on the couch, and spilling onto the floor. I was neither sick of the class, nor numb, nor in shock. I still cared and would continue to care. It had been a wonderful class, and Jessie's remark helped me to see many of its facets.

Teaching, as some of the books on my lap reminded me, should be student-centered. I agree. But if learning is the issue, then it can't just be about the students learning. I don't want to give the students a curriculum that is really mine, of course. They have their work to do and I want to help them do it; I'll do my work. But there *is* the matter of the teacher, too. In an airplane, flight attendants tell adults to put on their oxygen masks first before helping their children. You can't help your children breathe when you've allowed yourself to be asphyxiated. Just so, learning. The class was a success because the students learned and ended the semester wanting to learn more. They weren't the only ones. I, too, discovered and wanted to discover more. Teaching must not only be student-centered, it must also be about exploration. Which requires, I think, that the professor explore, too. And breathe. And relate how we're changing to the deepest challenges we all face as humans. When I become asphyxiated in the classroom, I hope I have the courage and creativity to do whatever it takes to begin breathing again or to abandon the classroom altogether. I can't help my students if I'm unconscious.

That Buddhism and the Environment class ended, but I couldn't stop talking about it. Finally, a friend suggested I write this book. These essays, then, grew from my reflections on my Buddhism and the Environment class, but they grew in directions I hadn't anticipated. I wondered self-consciously for the first time: what demands my attention as a Buddhist *and* as a teacher? I reflected on the implications of Buddhist practices on my teaching. I looked through the Buddhist texts with an eye to analyzing the ones most focused on teaching.[16] My topics here include anger, wonder, and compassion. I analyze the story of a serial killer who becomes a Buddhist monk and one about the Buddha facing a community dispute over a cup of water. I take a look at powerful metaphors from the Buddhist texts. The essays aren't uniform. They're not all from one point of view. My hope is that these varied essays circle around the parts of what makes teaching important and that they may bring some of us closer to a center that can hold, at least for a little while. Too often I find fellow teachers empty, worn out, and disengaged when our profession has at its roots a demand for meaning, vigor, and engagement. Too often teachers are urged to focus on measurable outcomes when so much of what makes life worth living and the world worth working on is immeasurable. I hope these essays, in all their variety and with their different approaches, bring readers to dynamic commitment to the best that is immeasurable.

CHAPTER I

Lie Until It's True

Attention in the Classroom

What a foe may do to a foe,
Or a hater to a hater—
Far worse than that
The mind ill held may do to him.
—*Dhammapada* 42

Buddhists prize meditation as the primary muscle of ethical action and spiritual knowledge. Through cultivating attention,[1] you learn to let go of what is not happening here and now so that extraneous motivations and ideas don't interfere with your direct perception of reality—you learn to let go of greed, anger, and delusion so they don't interfere with how you're perceiving and what you're doing. Instead, you perceive what is happening here and now, and greet it with generosity, loving-kindness, clarity and insight. Developing your power of attention simultaneously feels good, helps you to behave better, and makes your life more meaningful.

Like a muscle, the quality of attention can be developed through its use. As you practice paying attention to what is happening right here, right now, you become better able to pay attention. You strengthen your power of attention. It's like learning to play a piano—you practice hour after hour until you can play Mozart. In the case of attention, all that practice pays off, too. Hour after hour, you watch as physical feelings, emotions, thoughts, and inclinations arise and pass away. Every moment clusters of these arise and pass away. You practice noting their presence and letting them go. You watch them go, not allowing them, for this period of daily practice, to cause you to act. For now, they are just part of a parade to be watched. Later, let's say an acquaintance has come by and the two of you are having tea in your cherished cups with lovely silver trim and violets on them. Suppose your guest stumbles as he brings his cup to the next room. You leap to help him regain his stability, concerned that he might fall. You think nothing of your cup and the possibility of its crashing to the floor. That attention to the pain and comfort of another, the lack of concern for the gratification of one's own selfish desires, is Buddhism's playing of Mozart.[2]

Buddhists' reverence of attention is made clear in stories. One features a much-loved monk who was repeatedly frustrated that his eyes closed in meditation, helping send him off to sleep. He finally ripped off his eyelids to stay awake. It is said that where his eyelids landed the first tea plants grew, giving the gift of caffeine to those who yearn to cultivate attention. In one form of Buddhism, a person walks among meditators to offer strong and resounding blows across the upper back to bring dozing meditators back to the moment. For one month, I meditated daily at a temple of this sort. Thirty of us sat each morning and evening in a still room lit by just a few candles. For long stretches, we heard only the occasional candle flicker or the soft padding of the walker's socks on the floor. When that stick hit the back of someone, however, a loud thwack resounded, calling everyone to attention. Traditionally, the walker discerns who needs the blows by watching the meditators' postures for signs of distraction or sleep, but in that temple the meditator nonverbally requested the blow by putting her hands together in prayer position. Regardless of who determines who will be so dramatically brought back to attention, both the person who wields the stick and the person who receives the blow bow to the stick that has served to help a person keep the discipline of attention. I bowed to that discipline stick with the reverent gratitude I feel for everything that helps me attend properly.

These stories may seem violent and even disgusting, but they serve to emphasize the power of attention. According to Buddhists, with that power you can respond freely and skillfully to your intentions as they are rooted in generosity. Without powers of attention, you can only react, restricted by a limited view of what is and what can be, your intentions crippled by desire or anger. Your memories and fears for the future obscure your view and limit your response. The Buddha himself became the Buddha ("the enlightened one") through the wisdom he gained by paying attention. Buddhists understand that through proper attention everyone can become enlightened.

So I sit in formal meditation daily and practice paying attention, moment by moment, to what is happening, to what I am experiencing through my senses and in my mind. I recognize what Buddhists call the monkey quality of the mind—how it swings from tree to tree. This solitary daily training of noticing the monkey mind and of experiencing each moment and letting it go as it passes away can help teachers when they're in the classroom. They can then better resist getting lost in the comments of one student, in a short lecture they're giving, in their own desires and pains. When slighted by a student, a teacher may be more able to see past that slighting to the dynamics of what's going on—the intricacies of the teacher-student relationship, and our mutual teaching and learning.

Teachers have any number of problems related to attention. You woke up from a distressing nightmare. You cannot find any love for your profession, for your daily work. (Who cares about this subject to which you've devoted a fair portion of your life? Who cares about academics at all?) Your partner is leaving you. You are deeply and deliriously in love. Your cat is ill. You're now in class: how do you attend to what is really there?

The answer: you simply, repeatedly, call your attention back to whatever you are doing. Again and again and again.

Similarly, the students suffer attention problems. They woke up from awful nightmares. They cannot find any love for their work as students, for their daily work. (Who cares about these subjects of study? Who cares about academics at all?) Their partners broke up with them. They are in love. Their cats are ill. And if they're simply young, as my students are, they are riding chemical/hormonal trains that take them all over the universe within the space of an hour. How do they attend to what is really there?

You get the idea. Teachers need not try to keep students' attention as though it were a hostage. They are simply obliged to help them call their attention back again and again.[3] Teachers call the students to pay attention to what is going on. They want to bring the students back, gently, from wherever they are going. Teachers want to direct students' minds to whatever is in front of them.

Once a colleague ended class, enraged. The students didn't pay any attention at all when she spoke, they talked through class, ate snacks—why, they acted as though she weren't there at all. They were, she said, exceedingly disrespectful. Then she gave me a three-minute demonstration of the kind of lecture she gave in class, and I started to see the problem. What the teacher *said* and what she communicated with the rest of her body were opposites. It was hard to watch her when what was coming out of her mouth was being cancelled out by the rest of her body. She was saying (without any particular volume or changes in emphasis) some things about her area of specialty. Her body, on the other hand, was punishing anyone who paid attention to it. She wasn't making eye contact; her trunk didn't face me. Her arms and legs swung the way a three-year-old's do when it's time to go to bed but that toddler is reluctant to go.

It was clear: something in her didn't want attention.

Some days I don't want attention, either. All I want to do is stay home and read a book. If I must be with others, I want to do so wearing sunglasses. As to my colleague, the deep reflection she did after our discussion was helpful in discerning why she didn't want her students' attention, and I recommend that kind of reflection to anyone who finds they have the same problem. In the meantime, however, here are some specifics about getting people's attention when you're talking.

- First, simply reconcile yourself to getting some attention for a while in the service of communication. Face your students, take a deep breath and let it out, work on a smile that is both authentic and welcoming.
- Start class on time and thereby communicate to the students that every minute in the classroom is precious, every minute counts. (If you don't start on time regularly, you will find that a certain sluggishness, a certain reluctance, a heaviness creeps into the classroom. In a sense, you've taught that to the class.)
- Discern a particular point or two you're trying to make—either in your short lecture or during the class period. Then choose particular words/ideas to punch or emphasize, and emphasize these points. (Whisper, shout, vary your tone,

pause significantly before or after those words, make a particular unforgettable gesture when you speak those words, for example.) Repeat the points, changing the wording or keeping it the same while you make it more interesting some other way. Call on students to repeat those points periodically as you build on them—let them show you they're learning. (Make it a game, make it call-and-response.)

- Make eye contact with particular students as you speak so that eventually many if not all (depending on your class size) have had eye contact with you.
- Ask students questions frequently to make sure they're following you. For example, "Now, I have just said a few things about the mechanics of synapses. What were those things?" Take the time, make sure they get it right.
- Use diagrams, drawings, pictures. (When I am feeling shy, I use an overhead projector or PowerPoint. While students are facing me, their attention is deflected a bit to what's on the screen.)
- Avoid talking longer than you need in order to get your point across.
- Relate what you're doing in class to what they are actually attending to.

Before addressing how the Buddha did this latter on occasions, it's worth examining more closely the advice to avoid talking longer than necessary. Often when we speak, we feel good. We're doing something with our bodies and minds and that is moderately to greatly exciting. If we're talking about an area of interest, well, all the better. So as teachers we, understandably, tend to talk more. Add to this the complication that many of those to whom we speak every day are below us in status and power and so disinclined to interrupt us, and there's a set up for unfortunate monologues that bore everyone but the speaker. A linguist reports a story about the problems in communication between teachers and students, which she compares to those of parents and children. She audiotaped conferences between teachers and students and then met with each individually to get their impressions of how well they communicated: "One student said of a long monologue by her teacher: 'She is going on about something, but it would have been rude to interrupt. She clearly didn't hear what I said in the first place.' Of the same passage, the teacher reported, 'This is a teaching moment for me. I like these moments. . . . I can really teach here.'"[4]

This research embarrasses me as it affirms the adage: if the student hasn't learned, the teacher hasn't taught. What the teacher was doing in this case *felt* like teaching but wasn't. Attention to this area of possible self-delusion can help teachers speak in a way worth listening to.

So far I have discussed the more obvious elements of getting the attention of students. Other aspects of this process are more subtle—such as using what students are already attending to, as the Buddha did on many occasions. For example, once a group of young men stumbled upon the Buddha in the woods while they were chasing a prostitute who had stolen something of theirs. When they asked him if he'd seen a woman, the Buddha asked, "Which is better for you, that you should seek a woman or that you should seek yourselves?" When they agreed that it would be better if they seek themselves, he invited them to sit and listen to the Dhamma (Buddhist teaching).[5] (Would that our own students could so easily be turned from their various pursuits to listen to a teaching.) A bit school-marmy and pedantic in the modern American setting, I think, but the point is clear: it's helpful to relate what students are drawn to to what you are all doing in class together.

The complex results that can come of relating teaching to students' other interests are apparent in another story. In this one, the Buddha heard that one of his followers, Nanda, was thinking of disrobing as a monk and rejoining the larger community—in essence, of giving up his studies. When the Buddha asked why, Nanda replied, "When I left to renounce the house life, the [. . .] beauty Janapadakalyāṇī gazed after me with her hair partly held back and she said, 'Come back soon, prince.' When I remember that, I lead the holy life dissatisfied."[6] Well, no wonder.

The Buddha knew what Nanda needed. He took him to look at "five hundred nymphs with dove's feet" and asked Nanda to compare their beauty with that of Janapadakalyāṇī. Nanda could hardly compare them, the nymphs were so much more beautiful: "Janapadakalyāṇī is like a scalded she-monkey with her nose and ears lopped off compared to these five hundred nymphs with dove's feet," he said. "She does not count at all; she is nothing like them; there is no comparison whatever."[7] The Buddha then made a promise: if Nanda kept on with the holy life, he'd get five hundred nymphs with dove's feet.

All very well, but the other monks were not impressed with Nanda's new motivation for the holy life. They "treated him as a hireling who had sold himself." Humiliated, he retired and practiced with diligence until he was enlightened. (No longer desirous of the nymphs, Nanda returned to the Buddha to release him from his vow. But the Buddha was one step ahead of him. When he saw that Nanda's heart "was freed from taints," he knew he was free from keeping that promise.) Under the Buddha's guidance (and notably with the help of his fellows ostracizing him), Nanda's attraction to a beautiful woman was transformed into an impetus for practice.

When students stop learning in a regular high school or college, it is often because they hope for something better in another context—a different kind of learning, money, a beautiful man or woman. That something better, they feel, will make their lives more meaningful, more purposeful. But will it? Two lines of thought come to mind. One is simply that regardless of what their hearts quicken after, if we don't know it, we can't help them. To learn about their hopes, we can simply ask the students what they're thinking about—one-by-one, in small groups, over coffee, before class, anonymously on index cards. If we don't know about Janapadakalyāṇī, we don't know to show them the 500 nymphs with dove's feet.

The other line of thought is more complex. I am concerned about what our students really learn in our schools. If, as Cesar Chavez says and as I believe, "The end of all education should surely be service to others," are we doing our jobs? Do students in our schools really learn what they need to be of service to others? The world has too many poor, sick, dying people and poor, sick, dying ecosystems. Do our classes and curricula direct students to this suffering and teach them how to alleviate it? Or do our schools instead socialize them into a certain level of comfort or resign them to a lack of thereof? While I cannot call for a complete revision of our educational system, I am convinced that one way teachers can remain vital is to keep these questions in mind.

Some students are compelled by a desire to serve others, but others want the nymphs. For some students, the A's at the top of our grading scale are their dove-footed nymphs. Most of my students are quite compelled by grades. They are aiming for careers, and their grades are their highways to these careers. The education I provide, then, must help them understand that mere careers aren't enough. Their learning needs to be designed so they experience their own pain and the pain of those around them in such a way that they are called to alleviate pain as much as they can.

While it's important to know what motivates students, it's also critical for me as a teacher to know what motivates me. For example, I frequently use new material in class. At the beginning of the term, for any particular class, I have never read about one third of the assignments, sometimes more. For a long time I admitted this infrequently, but the main reason for my practice is not laziness—it's a way I keep courses interesting for myself, cultivating a curiosity that is real and vibrant during class. It motivates me. It gives my classes an edge. By facing unforeseen problems, I've been forced to improvise creatively, and students and I have learned a lot of things not on the syllabus.[8]

In my first year of teaching I assigned a particularly poorly written and difficult article I'd never read. I didn't read it until the day before class, and when I did, I was appalled. My students were sure to come to class resentful and angry, not having understood so much as the main point of the article. This was going to a pedagogical disaster. What were we going to do? Into a basket went some wads made up of used paper, and as the students arrived I invited them each to take one or more. (How quickly the mood changed from resentment and anger to curiosity—no teacher had ever done this before, and they'd been in school for more than 12 years.) Then I announced that whenever they wanted to express their anger toward me for assigning such a horrendous article, they could let a paper ball fly at me with no ill consequences. The classroom filled with a playful mischievousness. Although they threatened me throughout the period, not a single paper ball came my way. Not until the very end, that is, when they all let fly. The flurry in those last few minutes was a celebration of our accomplishments that hour rather than a miserable complaint about their reading.

I've gotten better at discerning the appropriateness of readings from a glance so my students don't suffer dramatically as they did during those first years. Nevertheless, on another occasion I managed to assign an entire book that was packed with material, far more than the students could absorb in the short time we had. When the problem became clear, we had a brainstorming session that led to, among other things, a ten-minute presentation on skimming—how to get the main points quickly by reading the table of contents, the headings and subheadings, and paying particular attention to introductions and conclusions, as well as first and last sentences in paragraphs. Skimming, obviously, is not always or even often a good alternative to a careful reading of a textbook, but it's a good skill to have and can be useful for review.

Even when I've chosen a lively, fascinating essay, my students still have trouble focusing. If I know they're overwhelmed by the work in my class, the problems in the world, the problems on campus (any time from midterms on generally seems appropriate), I instigate a whining session. I visibly set a timer for five minutes and invite the students to use the time to call out their greatest annoyances. As students try to top each other with their annoyances, they become energized. Occasionally students just need to let you know their current problems and issues, and sometimes it's more effective to listen to them on topics completely unrelated to the class than it is to storm ahead assuming they have what they need to follow you. They don't. They need motivation to follow a teacher, and leaving them and their concerns behind tells them the teacher values something else more than them. By ignoring their need for motivation, she's created a disinclination to follow her. Five minutes can clear the air for serious and important work, inform the teacher of students' problems, raise the class energy level, and focus the students. You may be concerned that the students will take this opportunity to dump on the teacher and the class. It's true; they can. In many cases, however, if a student starts to do this and the teacher does not react defensively but simply listens, another student or two will defend the class. Either way, though, whether students come to the defense or not, you've learned something valuable and you do have the timer on your side. You can address the complaints later as you like. I suggest waiting at least one day before replying if at all.

Not that all student concerns can be attended to. Not even most of them. In fact, valuable lessons can be learned when students find what professors won't attend to, what teachers ignore. Once while living on a Sri Lankan island, I spotted offshore an outrigger canoe holding two Sri Lankans and a Caucasian man. My curiosity was piqued—the only nearby island was an island monastery like ours, only for men. Were these men headed to that island? Was there to be a westerner practicing Buddhism on that island? At that moment, Sister Khema, the abbess of the nunnery, happened by. "Hey," I called to her, "There's a white man in a boat out there. Do we know anything about white men in boats?"

"It doesn't matter," she replied, not pausing in her walk.

In a regular classroom, the teacher can say, "OK: Five minutes about your parking troubles, your bodily woes, and your negative interactions with others and then back to our topic in the long term interest of your contributing helpfully to the world despite your distractions." The teacher in this way simultaneously gives importance to particular woes of students while communicating their greater responsibility to others.

Instead of listening to his monks whine, the Buddha sometimes used miracles to get their attention. At one point he "rose into the air to the height of seven palm-trees, and project[ed] a beam for the height of another seven so that it blazed and shed fragrance, and then reappeared in the Gabled Hall of the Great Fast."[9] A professor of mine once brought in a piano and led our entire class in a song about the founders of the field of psychology—miracle enough in those circumstances. If you're capable of such feats and can use them to help students attend, do so.

A one-on-one conversation with a student can miraculously remove obstacles that promise only to get larger as the term wears on and nerves fray. Once I had a senior, Beth, taking a 100-level class who behaved quite immaturely in class—criticizing other students by making faces at her friends, rolling her eyes, shifting angrily in her seat—basically acting as though she were above and outside the challenges of our classroom. Beth had disengaged from most members of the class and from our work and struck out with a few friends to mock the whole proceedings. I didn't know Beth—I'd never had her in a class before—but her behavior was not helping the class. My teaching mentor Roger Betsworth advised me to guide her in a certain kind of conversation.[10] I called her into my office and outlined how we would proceed: "I'd like to have a frank conversation about your performance in the class. First I'm going to tell you some things I see in your behavior, then I'm going to tell you what those things seem to communicate to me. Then I'm going to ask you to offer your reflections on the situation. Don't worry: you will get your say." I then described specific occasions when her behavior had seemed disrespectful. I was quite specific and did not burden my telling with the emotions I actually felt, which were anger and frustration. I concluded, "Frankly, this behavior makes me think you've forgotten you're in college. You act like you're in high school."[11]

She looked at me, stunned. There was a long silence.

"I had no idea you could tell how I felt," she replied, and I watched as she figured out the roots of the problem, her face opening up as she considered what I'd told her. She said she was behaving that way because it seemed as though in that class she *was* back in high school. As a senior, she'd learned to work hard in her classes and enjoy the work. But she felt a lot of students in the class were not working as hard—they were first-years and hadn't learned what she felt she had about working seriously. She reminisced that she had gone to a bad high school and lots of students had treated the work disrespectfully. Now that she was back with underclass students, she felt as though she were back in high school, and "I guess I act just like I feel." Her honesty lit up the room. We'd made a lot of progress in a short period of time. And it was clear we were going to have some concrete ways to solve our problems shortly.

"So, what's the solution?" I asked her. "It sounds like there are some things I need to do as the professor and some things you need to do as a student." From that point we had a constructive conversation about ways I could help the less serious students work more seriously and specific ways she could behave to help foster the learning environment we both wanted. We were on the same team solving a problem together that affected us both. My anger and frustration dissipated, and I sensed none from her. This conversation transformed anger into helpful self-reflection and student-teacher collaboration.

The Buddha's miracles were more dramatic, but the miracle of breaking down barriers of status, disrespect, and lack of attention can be pretty dramatic too—and they are the kind of work the Buddha valued. Ironically, considering the drama of some of his own, he actually warned against showy miracles. They don't really convince skeptics and they don't focus onlookers on the important issue of relieving suffering.

Of course I like to discover problems with students and work with them to formulate ways of handling them, but with some students that seems impossible. They condemn a professor's openness and interest in collaboration as signs of weakness and ignorance. In the face of innovative interactive classroom exercises, for example, such a student wants a lecture from an authority: "Why don't you just *teach* me if you know so much?" (After all, most students have been trained to *receive information* from teachers, not to grapple with their teachers and fellows to *create knowledge*.)[12] If a teacher doesn't lecture, these students assume, it must be because that teacher doesn't know much. According to the Buddhist texts, the Buddha once faced a similar situation when he came to a place where Kassapa, who thought he himself was the accomplished spiritual master, was teaching. Knowing Kassapa's arrogance was only leading him to refuse learning offered by the Buddha, the Buddha sought to get Kassapa's attention and earn his respect. First, the Buddha defeated a horrible snake demon who had "supernormal powers [and] who [was] venomous, fearfully poisonous" without killing it. This defeat impressed the gods so much that they came and paid homage to him. Trees, similarly impressed, bent their branches down so the Buddha could wash out a rag by a river with less trouble. The Buddha evidenced power, and beings recognized that power in all manners of ways. Still, however, Kassapa thought he was more spiritually advanced than the Buddha and was unwilling and unable to learn from him. Finally, faced with this level of obtuseness, the Buddha gave Kassapa a helpful shock by saying to him, "There is nothing that you do by which you might become an Arahant (an enlightened one) or enter into the way to becoming one."[13]

Kassapa prostrated himself to the Buddha right then and there and asked to go forth, to become a monk.[14, 15] (Becoming a Buddhist monk or nun is called "going forth" from the longer phrase "going forth from home to homelessness.")

I am uncomfortable with this sort of bully-teaching, and I'm hesitant to recommend it. For one thing, it happens enough already. Teaching in most traditional contexts already reinforces violent habits and oppressive power structures in so many ways that I'm troubled by any self-conscious reinforcement of these patterns. The Buddha, however, was spiritually accomplished. Presumably, with enlightenment, his motivations were much better than mine are going to be in this lifetime, so, from a Buddhist perspective, he could be more skillful than I could with this technique. I've only done this sort of bullying once to good effect.[16] In my case I had a student who had been quite rude at the end of the previous semester—disrespectful of our class and our class time. Once he came into class and lay down on top of a table with a huge sigh, calling everyone's attention away from the work at hand and to his own misery. New to teaching, I had foolishly chosen to ignore his behavior because the student intimidated me and because the semester was ending soon. When the young man showed up in another of my classes the next semester, I was surprised—I thought his rudeness had indicated he didn't appreciate my classes and wouldn't take another. He was rude repeatedly in much more subtle ways in this new class.

Having been coached by my mentor, I took that student outside the class directly after one such incident, when he seemed to be making a comment about me to a fellow student. In the hall, shaking with anger and standing too close to him, I asked him directly and forcefully what was going on. My physical stance with him was unyielding. When he looked confused, I described what I'd seen and speculated he had been making a derogatory comment about me. He was stunned and sputtered that he'd noticed I neither called on him nor visited his group when I was working with small groups and that he was noting this to his fellow student. "Do you think that is a very helpful way of dealing with your problem?" I asked. Greeted with silence, I suggested that he could take me aside and point out that behavior and ask about it as I was asking about his behavior now. That, I told him, would have a better effect than simply behaving in a manner I could only interpret as being rude. I told him I would try to pay more attention to whatever group he was in and I expected him to be more polite and direct.

The young man and I were able to work out a mutually respectful relationship, so one could say bullying him worked. He was able to learn and I was able to teach. Our relationship got better, too. Perhaps I gave him more possibilities of response to this sort of problem than simply talking behind a person's back. I'm still not comfortable with it, though. While the Buddha might have managed to confront Kassapa without anger and fear, treasuring the goal of Kassapa's release from the round of suffering, I was primarily motivated by fear of what this student could do to my class. I was not motivated by generosity and love, as Buddhist philosophy encourages and which I've found to be better compasses for navigation. While I certainly was not even close to being out of control with anger or fear (in fact, the event was carefully choreographed), my motivations were far from what I dream they someday might be.

A larger issue related to this young man's problem is the need of some students for a lot of attention. When he had lain down on that table in class, that student had wanted attention. When he talked with his fellow student, he wanted attention. To his mind (and probably in reality, too, in this case), I had been ignoring him. Why would I ever withhold attention from a student who wanted it? Generally speaking, if a student wants attention, I try to give it, and I try to give more positive attention than I managed in this case. Why not? Too often in the face of a student's need for attention a teacher will dismiss that need with a comment such as, "Oh, he just wants attention." That sentence is code for "There's no real reason to give this person what he wants." If all he wants is attention, though, there's no reason not to give it. After all, to attend to means to care for. And teachers are to care for their students. If I knew a student behaved annoyingly because she was hungry, would I pointedly ignore the hunger in the same way? I hope not. I hope I would offer the student some food. To dismiss a problem like that is to make myself callous and deny myself the pleasure of watching a hunger satisfied, of experiencing joy in the pleasure another takes in food. I regret that many of us teach students who are desperate for attention—we cannot fill all those needs. But giving care as we can to those who need it is feeding the hungry: a valuable thing to do. As a general rule, if a student wants care, one should probably be attentive to that student—when and in what form that attention comes is part of the pedagogical art.

At all times when I teach, I try to attend. I try to be aware of where I am, who I'm with, what I'm doing. I try to be aware of what I see, hear, smell, taste, feel. I try to be aware of the dynamism of being with others doing something important. I find as I practice being present outside the classroom, I'm much more present in the classroom. So I work to be with my students. At the beginning of class, I look around at my group and smile to myself: what adventures we'll have today together. Why, we haven't got a clue what's going to happen.

During class, I attend to each student who speaks, helping the other students to do that, too. I make sure they make eye contact with the speaker. (Sometimes if it requires students turning their necks or turning their whole trunks, they won't do it. Years of classroom training keeps them static. One can use their natural inclination to keep their eyes on you more than on their fellow students by walking over to whoever is speaking and standing right by her. More direct approaches work, too—just ask everyone to turn to look at the speaker and point out how the movement energizes them a bit and how making eye contact helps keep their attention on the speaker.) I try to be aware of those who are fading away and help them come back—if I thought someone on the opposite team is not paying attention in volleyball, I'd head the ball their way, of course. This makes for a good game, good competition. There's less competition in my classroom—I hope it's more of a creative building process—but I make sure to toss the volleyball to the people who need some help focusing. I knew a teacher who could lead a conversation with fifty students participating—I'm still working toward that goal.[17]

So far in this chapter I've used the term attention in a broad sense. In Buddhist philosophy, however, there is what one teacher of mine referred to as a "science" of meditation. Other books address this topic at greater length, but here I just note this: many students in the United States don't notice how good it feels simply to pay attention to something. So many aspects of their lives give such immediate emotional and physical rewards that they simply don't realize consciously that the intellectual engagement required to work on an algebra problem or read a difficult text is rewarding in and of itself. Calling students' attention to this subtle good feeling can give them a bit more impetus to do any intellectual work.

Related to the intrinsic rewards of attention are other rewards one can gain through different kinds of attention. Buddhist texts offer a wide variety of methods of attention (or meditation, cultivation), but regardless of which ones a person engages in, all can help to enlarge one's sensibilities and deepen one's heart. Like the practice of reading, meditation demands you remove yourself from the nexus causing emotions and from the tumult of emotions themselves. Removed from emotions, one isn't paralyzed by them. One isn't tossed about on the seas or running desperately for shore. Nor does one act on them overly hastily or distractedly. Yet one still *cares* about them, giving them calm, quiet attention.[18]

When I was in that Sri Lankan island nunnery, I spent three months meditating between six and fourteen hours a day. The air was wonderfully humid but cool. The sounds of the palms of coconut trees wisping together filled my days and nights. And I loved the food. We had rice every day at lunch, and the curries were delicious. We ate juicy papayas, mangosteins, rambutans, and other tropical fruit. Further, we only ate two meals a day, spending eighteen and a half hours a day without food (as is the custom of Theravada Buddhist renunciants).[19] Because of these reasons, and because I was young and fit and metabolizing food quickly, mealtimes were wondrous for me. I ate the food with vigor. Yet each day I was required to chant this reminder before I ate:

> Reflecting carefully, I eat this food. Not for amusement or intoxication, not for the sake of physical beauty and attractiveness, but only for the endurance and continuance of this body, for ending discomfort, and for assisting the holy life, considering: "Thus I shall terminate old feelings without arousing new feelings and I shall be healthy and blameless and live in comfort."[20]

Having taken the five precepts, which included a vow prohibiting me from untruthfulness, I was troubled that every time I chanted, I was lying. I was definitely eating the food for sensual pleasure. When I approached the abbess (another one of my finest teachers), she let a pause yawn as she looked me dead in the eye. She replied, "Lie until it's true."[21]

Attend as much as you can. Pay close attention in class, to your work, to grading, to each student who comes to your office or passes you in the hall. And if you feel disconnected, if you feel alienated, if you are tired and just want to curl up by a fire with a book and forget this whole thing, if you feel like this is the biggest waste of time in the universe, try to pay attention anyway. And if you're angry, if all the students, the administration, your colleagues are all clearly plotting your demise, try to pay attention. But if you can't, pretend. Pretend you're attending. Pretend this is the most important moment in your life and in that of your students. Pretend that this thing called a classroom is a crucible. Pretend that we all breathe to be together doing this.

Until it's true.

CHAPTER 2

Viewing Each Other
with Kindly Eyes

Community in the Classroom

*I hope that you are all living in concord, with mutual appreciation, without
disputing, blending like milk and water, viewing each other with kindly eyes.*
—*Majjhima Nikāya* 128.11

My dream for the students in any of my classes is that they have
a safe environment in which they can explore important questions respectfully with others. I strive, then, to form a community
in the classroom. But, really, why bother? Does a "community"
of learning really help students learn? And what makes a "community" a "community" anyway? One particular Buddhist text,
The Quarrel at Kosambī, reveals many community- and
learning-related issues and gives a charming view of the Buddha
working on them. The story also indicates why a supportive
community can help learning.[1]

Like many religious stories, The Quarrel at Kosambī is complex, and different aspects of the text are illuminated depending
on what the reader brings to it. Later in this chapter I share more
details of the story as I analyze it, but first, to give an overview,
here is a summary of the plot: One day a teacher-monk left a container of clean water in a monastery bathroom by mistake. (Why
the clean water might be an offense is not explained in the text,
but we can infer he didn't flush the toilet after using it.[2]) When
confronted by another teacher-monk, he apologized and was
told it was OK—the action wasn't really an offense because he'd
been ignorant of the rules. Later, though, his accuser vacillated:

now leaving the water there *had* been an offense. Not only that, but the accuser told his students about the foolish and wayward actions of the water-leaving monk. The two teacher-monks and their students then fought over whether an offense had been committed and whether the monk should be suspended.

Seeking to end the community turmoil, the Buddha offered some advice, but the intensity of the disagreements continued to rise and drove him into solitude. Finally the two groups came together and, amidst much confusion, resolved the difficulty. The offending monk admitted his error and was readmitted as a monk.

What was the ultimate cause of the problem? One monk leaving a container of water in the wrong place? Another monk obsessing about rules? Both gossiping to students? All these elements contributed to the problem, but it's unclear initially which are the significant ones.

The Buddha: Everyone is an Integral Member of the Group

One good way to find the most significant root problems is to examine how the Buddha seeks to solve them before being driven into solitude. As the story unfolds in the original text, readers see that upon learning about the dispute between the two teachers and their students, the Buddha speaks with the monks on each side of the controversy and reminds them of where they may have gone wrong in the incident. Then he shows them their losses in this particular controversy. After all, if they suspend the monk, *their group would be lessened*. They lose that member of the group, which is then integrally different. All the experiences of being part of that group change, too. (For example, the Buddha points out that in small and large events, in daily and annual events, the group will be less because one monk from it is suspended.) The Buddha also invites the monks to appreciate the accused and accuser monks' learning and their commitment to further learning.

The Buddha here indicates that a community is created by those in it—every single one of them. Honoring this in my own classroom, I try to encourage my students to value each member of the class from the first day and consistently throughout the semester. I use short periods of class time over the first several weeks to ensure that each person in the room knows the names of every other person in the class.[3] I also focus our attention on the material and the joys of working with it together. On the first day of class we jump right in and do some kind of mini-project related to what we will study. *After* we engage and work cooperatively together, and thus *after* students have learned something and had the pleasure of getting to know each other a bit, I distribute syllabi. This happens at the end of the first hour, when their attention has already been focused on their work and they've attended together and benefited from that. I have not become the center of their attention; I have not become a rule-enforcer.

Another way I help students value each other, as the Buddha advises his monks to do, is to encourage students to recognize and socialize with each other outside class. I note out loud in class the power of cliques and encourage students to befriend students in other cliques—to cross those boundaries. I dramatize the point—if I showed up at one of their parties, would they ignore me? After all the interesting conversations we've had together in class, would they utterly ignore that we have a relationship? Why? What does that mean? What are the implications of that?

Some teachers ignore students' social worlds (and even denigrate those who attend to these worlds as inappropriately involved), but humans (students, in this case) rightfully attend to the people around them. After all, they are critically important to our happiness. The people around college- and high school-aged students may play an even more crucial role in their happiness because the human cognitive development at this age depends critically on social interactions. Why wouldn't teachers build in-class learning on this solid foundation of the need for friendship?

I emphasize the integrity of our community when I recognize repeated absences of a student as losses to all of us, not just to the missing student. If I know a student is sick, I invite members of the class to check on her, to call and ask if they can help. During one semester, when a student's sibling died and he left to be with his family, I brought a card to class and each of his classmates and I signed the card for him. That student's loss was our loss—out of compassion and honesty, we recognized that in a community action: the signing of a card.

By attending to these issues and encouraging students to recognize the fullness of their social lives in and beyond the classroom, I risk being dismissed as touchy-feely. I still worry the gesture of sending a condolence card from the class will be perceived as suitable more for second-graders than college students. It is, however, a kind and thoughtful thing to do, and I'd like my students to become kind and thoughtful, if they aren't already. Further, studies indicate that students' significant learning experiences come from their friends rather than books. One might as well use the class as an opportunity to make friends for learning.

While I nurture relationships between students, I also cultivate my own relationships with them. I invite a student (usually one who is sullen or quiet in class) out to lunch or for coffee for one-on-one socializing when I can. It doesn't matter what we talk about as long as we learn a bit more about each other and how we each view the world. I do not have the time to take each of my students out for coffee, but I can take a few, and that can help—it helps us recognize each other as multi-dimensional humans working together to accomplish something rather than as problems for each other. It helps us face rather than dismiss each other.

Again, I take risks when I do this sort of thing. Recently a colleague referred to my inviting students out to lunch as "sucking up to them." Ouch. But this reductive evaluation ignores the importance of maintaining good relationships. I don't think I should refrain from being kind to my students, from being attentive and concerned about their welfare, from doing what I can to have good relationships with them because some people will perceive my actions negatively. Trying to be concerned, compassionate, responsive, and working to encourage harmonious relationships is good practice. (Perhaps my colleague's comment on my efforts with students is a call for me to work similarly hard with my fellow faculty members.) Of course, some teachers find this sort of fraternizing unhelpful and uncomfortable. It's just not how they do things. There are other ways to maintain and deepen relationships with students that may be more natural for them: merely showing a film for extra credit and attending it with the students or catching a member of the class after an event related to one's field and casually talking with her about it are other ways to encourage harmony.

Let's get back to the story of the quarreling monks of Kosambī. Another critical element of the story revealed in the text is the Buddha's lack of interest in finding fault, in blaming, or even in determining what is just. When the Buddha asks the monks who found the water-leaving offensive to reflect on their actions, he doesn't ask them to decide who was right. Rather, he invites them to find fault in their own reasoning. He asks them to feel, explore, and imagine that monk's small and large contributions to the group and anticipate what they'd lose by suspending him. Assigning blame isn't important. Rather, it's important to recognize the contributions of specific individuals to the group, the unique qualities of the group, and group coherence.

In the text, when the Buddha approaches the group of monks who side with the suspended monk, he emphasizes the same points to them. In the modern classroom, these kinds of spontaneous reflections on individual gifts and group qualities can help students cultivate appreciation for those around them and for the best aspects of formal education. On a side note, the Buddha was understandably not interested in justice. Because his enlightenment included understanding karmic law, he knew justice would be served because that is how the universe works. The work of humans (in the Buddhist conception) is not to ensure justice but to cultivate wisdom and compassion. (See chapter 3 for more on karmic law and justice.)

Milk and Water: Harmonious Groups

In the Kosambī text, even after the Buddha speaks to the monks and reasons with them, they continue to quarrel. The Buddha then approaches the problem in another way: he finds a group of monks who get along harmoniously and asks them how they live "in concord, with mutual appreciation, without disputing, blending like milk and water, viewing each other with kindly eyes."4 (Here the Buddha learns from his followers, something that happens frequently in the texts. See chapter 6.) One of them replies,

As to that, I think thus: 'It is a gain for me, it is a great gain for me that I am living with such companions in the holy life.' I maintain bodily acts of loving-kindness towards these venerable ones both openly and privately; I maintain verbal acts of loving-kindness towards them both openly and privately; I maintain mental acts of loving-kindness towards them both openly and privately. I consider: 'Why should I not set aside what I wish to do and do what these venerable ones wish to do?' Then I set aside what I wish to do and do what these venerable ones wish to do. We are different in body, venerable sir, but one in mind.[5]

Those who live with him agree. They are grateful to each other and love and care for each other. When the Buddha asks how they were all "diligent, ardent and self-controlled," that same monk replies:

Lord, as to that, whichever of us returns first from the village with almsfood gets the seats ready, sets out the water for drinking and for washing and puts the refuse bucket in its place. Whichever of us returns last eats any food left over if he wishes; otherwise he throws it away where there is no grass or drops it into water where there is no life. He puts away the seats and the water for drinking and washing. He puts away the refuse bucket after washing it, and he sweeps out the refectory. Whoever notices that the pots of drinking water or washing water or water for the privy are low or empty sees to them. If any are too heavy for him, he beckons someone else by a sign of the hand and they move it by joining hands. We do not speak for that purpose. But every five days we sit out the night together in talk on the Dhamma [the Buddhist teachings]. It is in this way that we dwell diligent, ardent and self-controlled.

In short, the monks cultivate loving-kindness toward their fellows in their thoughts and in their deeds. They are considerate of each other's needs and do not speak except to enjoy the pleasures of talk about the Dhamma.

Teachers in today's classrooms can encourage similar appreciation among the students, nurturing learning communities. They can note how a student is helping all the class in its work and can thank that student. A teacher can also call attention to the unique conversations occurring in class and how they are dependent on the particular people in the class. When conversation gets nasty (my own field of study, religion, can certainly inspire defensiveness), teachers can invite a moment of silence and reflection. Aggressive, disrespectful, angry conversations do not energize a classroom without cost; they batter participants as well as listeners. Yes, students have and will continue to have aggressive conversations, but teachers can use class time to help them develop other more productive ways of communicating—ways that are less likely to inflict wounds and more likely to encourage communication, even with those who have very different viewpoints.

To cultivate kindness in another way, I sometimes teach students techniques to help them listen more deeply. A conversation on an explosive topic, for example, can polarize a class and grind useful discussion to a halt as students choose sides and attempt to argue down opposition. Concerned about that kind of polarization and paralysis, I once began a discussion on abortion by asking each person in the class, one by one, to answer the question: "What would you like everyone in this room to know about how you think and feel about abortion?" I had to coach the students on how to listen deeply, how to put aside their own interests and reactions and desires and instead commit themselves to the primary goal of understanding and empathizing with the speaker. It seemed to take a long time to listen to each person's views, but our discussion was careful and engaged and fruitful because students understood from the beginning that each student had complex emotions and opinions about the topic. Views could not be simplified; people and their emotions and thoughts could not be dismissed. Given what they'd learned in the first fifteen minutes of that class, their classmates could not be reduced to enemies holding offensive views.

The Buddha Takes Time Out

Returning to the text of the Kosambī story, we learn that after the Buddha tries to solve the dispute, he simply walks away from it. He concludes that the monks cannot be made to see the errors of their ways. The reader can feel his frustration as he ponders how people's voices rise in dispute but later these people don't understand how their own loud voices make the argument worse. He reflects further that hate never brings amity but rather amity brings amity. He asks, seemingly desperately, if even murderers and beasts can act in concord, why can't monks? Finally, the Buddha considers the advantages of going on alone:

> If you can find a trustworthy companion with whom to walk, both virtuous and steadfast, then walk with him content and mindfully, overcoming any threat of danger. If you can find no trustworthy companion with whom to walk, both virtuous and steadfast, then, as a king who leaves a vanquished kingdom, walk like a tusker in the woods alone. Better it is to walk alone: There is no fellowship with fools. Walk alone, harm none, and know no conflict; be like a tusker in the woods alone.[6]

And so he goes on retreat, living at the foot of a tree. He revels in the ease and peace and comfort he can enjoy alone, and when an elephant approaches, similarly troubled by other elephants, the two come to enjoy each other's company in a different sort of solitude—one that admits only two members, each of a different species. At one lovely moment, the Buddha reads the elephant's mind and exclaims, "Tusker agrees with tusker here; the elephant with tusks as long as shafts delights alone in woods: their hearts are thus in harmony."[7]

Can a teacher "be like a tusker in the woods alone"? Yes, in obvious and less obvious ways. Obviously if you have a life of a certain sort (with few primary care duties for humans and animals, for example) any time you're not teaching can allow solitude. Less obviously, a teacher spontaneously and publicly recognizing an immediate need for solitude can be world-altering for students. In the midst of an impassioned but then cruel debate, the teacher raises his hands in the air, his eyebrows high, an expression of surprise on his face. Students become silent and attend to him. He notes the high emotions and recognizes their value in signaling important issues. He also notes that such high emotions can interfere with good thinking and careful responding and suggests everyone spend a few minutes reflecting on the most important aspect of the issue for them. Two minutes later (when the teacher calls on students to create a list of the important aspects of the issue) the discussion continues—richer in *thought*, happily poorer in anger and cruelty. Or a teacher recognizes her own emotions as high and interfering with her conducting a class. She turns to the students and says, "Whew—I am so full of emotion I'm sure to say something I'll regret. I'm going to step outside for about one minute here, and then we will resume our conversation." She steps out, does what she can to calm herself, and returns to the class. In this way she models another way to handle high emotions: a temporary retreat. Sometimes timeout is good for everyone.

In examining these more detailed approaches to resolving the Kosambī argument, we see it isn't just one problem—it isn't simply that the monks aren't getting along. It is also that the Buddha's calm is disturbed by the monks. That's a crucial detail because when the Buddha retreats, he hasn't solved the difficulty. He just takes a break, letting the monks continue their annoying behavior. There are four parts, then, to the quandary: the lack of harmony in the monks' relations, how annoying that lack of harmony was to the Buddha, the Buddha's ignorance about how other monks live more harmoniously together, and his initial failure to encourage harmony in this case.

Surely any teacher can appreciate this more detailed examination of the dilemmas in the situation. It's one thing if students don't get along—it's something else if that annoys the teacher. There's a difference, too, between a teacher trying to solve a problem and failing and a teacher lacking what he or she needs to solve the problem. One time I was working with some students who did good work and got along fine. They didn't particularly enjoy each other, but neither were they in any way nasty or unproductive. I, however, was repeatedly troubled by how little I knew the students I was working with and how dry and bureaucratic (as opposed to stimulating and creative) my work with them felt. I had been involved with a similar group of students the year before and things had gone swimmingly. I wondered repeatedly, what was wrong with this new group? Finally, I had to conclude that there was nothing wrong with the group. I was the problem: I wanted them to be last year's group. I found I could do two things simultaneously to help the situation: (1) repeatedly let go of my desire to feel closer to these students—to have relationships with them like the ones I had enjoyed the previous year, and (2) foster some more closeness by inviting a few students to lunch for one-on-one conversations on any topic at all. When I'm annoyed with a class, there may be roots in the students' innocent errors. But the fault could as easily lie with me. In this particular case, I had to let my own desires die.

Who Ultimately Solves the Problem and How

After we watch the Buddha reveling in solitude, the Kosambī text surprises us because the integral participants now are neither the Buddha nor the monks. Who brings the situation to a new crisis after the Buddha goes away in defeat? The lay people of Kosambī, who are angry the Buddha was driven away by the monks' quarreling. These lay followers spurn the monks, refusing to offer them their usual respect and, significantly, almsfood, on which the monks depend for their lives. In response to this, the monks decide they'd better resolve their argument in front of the Buddha.

The allegiance of the lay followers to the Buddha invites a short meditation on perspective here. Many teachers, especially those in their early years, allow their perception of students and class dynamics to become skewed in the face of difficult classroom community issues. Often we think a whole class is going badly because one student makes impolite, loud, unhelpful comments. While that student might not be getting much from the class, how many others are there in the room? And how badly do they wish the offending student would just be quiet so everyone could do the work at hand? Often we attribute a class problem to one student and wish that student would just be ill or take a few days off or even withdraw from the class. While this sort of obsessing and demonizing is quite natural and common, focusing on one student as the locus of all problems is unfair to the student and unfair to the class. It simplifies complex dynamics and helps no one. I find that my (often subtle) behavior against students I demonize keeps the entire class, including myself, in a frustrating cycle. It limits my perceptions and reduces class creativity. When things go wrong, I am too quick to blame that student. During discussions, I too easily dismiss that student's reflections. My behaviors increase the alienation and negativity of the student, which in turn . . .

Two good ways to escape this trap—or avoid it in the first place—are one-on-one talks with students and loving-kindness meditation. The latter can take a variety of forms. One can simply visualize black clouds (the world's greed, anger, and delusion) being breathed in, and clear air (generosity, loving-kindness and compassion, clarity and understanding) being breathed out. One can simply repeat the phrase: "May [the name of the student] be peaceful and happy." The Buddhist texts advise different versions of this meditation depending on the circumstances, but a good basic one works this way: begin by sending loving-kindness to yourself. ("May I be peaceful and happy.") Then send it to a benefactor, someone who has only done good for you with no expectation of reward (so not a parent or lover—that's too complicated). From there, move on to a person for whom you have neutral feelings (go ahead, try to find one—this is often the most difficult part of this kind of meditation). Finally repeat your phrase or draw your attention to the person to whom you currently have negative emotions.[8]

After too many instances of allowing my emotions about a disruptive student to derail my classes, I tried practicing loving-kindness meditation. Now I do so regularly. Strangely, even now, after years of practicing loving-kindness meditation in relation to my work as a teacher, I'm amazed at how long I can remain annoyed and angry before I realize that my negative thoughts about a particular student can be seen as a cue to send them loving-kindness. Sometimes day after day I sit down to do loving-kindness meditation and though all my discursive thoughts are about that one student, I am too dull-witted from my obsessive anger to think to send that student loving-kindness. When I do remember, I find later I am more likely to notice good behavior and helpful contributions from that student. Also, of course, this meditation assists in conquering fear and hatred, which should never dominate a classroom, either from the perspective of the students or that of the professor.[9] (Can you believe I'm inviting teachers to do yet another teaching-related activity *on their own time*? Don't we all have enough to do? Yet these kinds of practices can alter the spirit with which one does one's work so significantly that work no longer feels like work. Imagine transforming your perspective so that all your teaching-related work fills your heart with joy.)

When the class looks like a complete mess wrought by a few students, the teacher often sees only the wreckage and feels despondent with his own lack of ability to handle it. Or he feels angry at those students, blaming them for all the problems. Both reactions ignore at least one important part of the larger picture: a group, such as the lay people of Kosambī, often includes quiet supporters of greater harmony. Most students want something useful and good to happen in the classroom, and most faculty members want to help them get it. The problems arise in the *how* of it all, and these problems are not merely the dilemmas of the teacher. Nor is the teacher necessarily the one who will solve them.

I see my students use their power to address such quandaries when they spurn a student they deem to be disruptive. When one or a group of students goes too far—be it a direction of inquiry or an attitude of meanness or whatever—the students show, often completely nonverbally, that this conversation or attitude is not what they came here for. They remove their own society from that of the "disruptive" student. Because I work largely with 18- to 21-year-olds, what a group may remove from another group isn't its physical nurturance but its social nurturance, and that has huge repercussions for those who are left isolated. As the lay people starved out the monks, so these students socially starve out their fellows. They stop looking at a certain student. They may roll their eyes or shift uncomfortably in their seats whenever she speaks. I watch for signs of this and invite students to speak carefully and frankly—sometimes in the classroom and sometimes out of it. In our current societal enthusiasm for derision and irony, I hate to encourage it, but scorning isn't necessarily a bad thing. It doesn't always need interrupting. It can be a group's way of taking a time-out. Rather than automatically squelching or automatically supporting shunning, one should be aware of the freeze-out and be careful in responding to it. If students spurn someone because of race, sex, class, sexual orientation, or other forms of dehumanization, the teacher does need to step in. Allowed to continue, this kind of practice ignores the humanity of the person(s) excluded. If students spurn someone because that person asks uncomfortable but helpful questions, the teacher also needs to step in and interrupt the cold reception. By doing so, the teacher helps the other students see that their discomfort can lead to learning, that the questions are good.

People who fight dehumanization sometimes have a hammer with which they want to pound every nail. They want to stop these kinds of dehumanizing comments from occurring by laying down the law such as, "I will not stand for that kind of comment in my classroom." This practice has merits. One oughtn't make dehumanizing comments, and that standard should be set in the classroom. I understand that inclination, engage in it sometimes, and am happy for it, but in my own teaching I more often like to recognize the complexity of the underlying problems that lead to this sort of comment and the possibility of students finding the problem and exploring it and of their need for time to do so. One can simply note the incident publicly as something to think about: "Hmmm, there's a lot of discomfort in the classroom right now and it seems to be a result of that last comment and the assumptions that underlie it." Or the teacher can go on to examine the cause of the rebuff more closely by writing the racist or sexist or otherwise dehumanizing comment on the board and inviting students to list the assumptions that underlie it. Students can be directed to free write about the comment and their responses to it. They can be invited simply to say one sentence about how they feel right then. Perhaps most significantly, the teacher can follow up on the problem the next time the class meets—indicating clearly that this isn't just a passing concern.

Keep to the Dhamma: Cultivating Loving-kindness, Generosity, Clarity, and Understanding

To return to the Kosambī text, another aspect of the story has to do with the advice the Buddha gives to all those who wonder how to treat the disputing monks. (The ones who shun the monks, after all, don't ask the Buddha what to do.) The Buddha's advice is concise: "Keep to the Dhamma."

This answer is deceptively easy. What is the dhamma in this regard?

The Buddha outlines eighteen ways one can discern what is not dhamma.[10] In essence, each of the eighteen ways (that include also "he shows a slight offense as a grave one and a grave offense as a slight one") calls upon the person him/herself to discern depending on his/her own knowledge and understanding of the dhamma. On the one hand, individual dhamma discernment is what caused the whole quarrel to begin with yet, on the other hand, it's all that we have at any given point—our understanding, based on our experience, of what is and is not true and helpful. At one point in the story, the Buddha's aunt, a nun, asks how to treat the disputing monks. With her, the Buddha is more explicit: "Hear the Dhamma from both sides, Gotamī. When you have done so, approve the views, the liking, the opinions and judgments of those who say what is Dhamma."[11] The Buddha's words apply to both teachers and students: Start where you are. Discern the world, listen to different views, and proceed as best you can in the best direction you can discern towards cultivating generosity, loving-kindness, compassion, clarity, and wisdom.

How, in the end, does the dispute come to a close? The monk who originally left the glass of water in the restroom comes to understand that indeed he was wrong and that the suspension is valid. Once the monk recognizes his error, the other monks can reinstate him, which they do. In the view offered by this part of the story, the whole event evolves from one person having some resistance, some stubbornness on the way to learning, and many speaking harshly.

No wonder the Buddha took refuge with his lone tusker friend!

Related Issues

So far I have concentrated on what the Kosambī text can contribute to understanding class communication. It's worth broadening the discussion now to see what other texts can contribute. There are too many to enumerate here—so I'll concentrate on a few.

A comparison can be made between classrooms (or universities or high schools) and monasteries, a comparison I've been interested in since I spent those four months in a Buddhist monastery in India. Just as a monastery can be a reasonably safe place to explore the possibilities of Buddhist practice and philosophy together, a classroom can provide a place where a cordial, cooperative group of people explores subjects and issues, where they practice learning and, I would argue, where they act in response to that learning. From its earliest days, Buddhist monasticism emphasized behavior over ideas. One could believe just about anything and still live together in the monastery. There was no creed. People's interior practices could be as different as night and day. For example, as Buddhism changed over time and different practices came to become popular and others receded, one meditating person might simply have attended to her breathing while another might have mentally built huge, detailed Buddha worlds in vibrant colors. Monks, nuns, and visitors only had to obey certain codes of behavior, most of which contributed to creating a calm atmosphere in which people could practice Buddhist meditation healthfully, could chant, care for others, and reflect on issues related to the Buddhist path. Those codes for monasteries included prohibitions against the deeply disturbing (such as urinating in the well) to the merely annoying and distracting (such as moving in jerky, fast, and uncontrolled ways).

According to the Buddhist texts, the Buddha decided communal living was aided by doing the following things in public and in private:

- showing loving-kindness to fellows in body, speech, thought,
- sharing with virtuous beings all gifts, including those of food,
- consistently keeping rules of conduct which lead to liberation and concentration, and persisting in liberation and concentration with fellows.[12]

Naturally, these are fine practices for the classroom. I like to emphasize the second point, that of generosity. What can I give to my students today other than the usual attention and planning for the classroom? Once I found a wonderful phrase in my reading, just a delightful phrase. So I wrote out the phrase on one side of 23 cards and wrote its definition and a sentence using it on the other side of those cards. I gave all the students in my class that semester the gift of the phrase. It became a focus of amusement for the rest of the semester and I ended up promising extra credit if they could work the phrase reasonably into their final papers. What the heck, it was a great phrase. ("Unquenchable ontological thirst" from Mircea Eliade's *The Sacred and the Profane: The Nature of Religion*.)

In another sutta (discourse, thread or record of a dialogue), the Buddha gives a similar list of qualities that aid communal living, except in this one, he begins by listing six roots of disputes that interfere with respect and deference toward the teacher, the dhamma, and the sangha. These roots lead to a monk's failure to fulfill the training, and the result is dispute, leading to the harm and unhappiness of many. These roots take hold when a monk

1. is angry and revengeful
2. is contemptuous and domineering
3. is envious and avaricious
4. is deceitful and fraudulent
5. has evil wishes and wrong views
6. adheres to his own views, holds them tenaciously and relinquishes them with difficulty[13]

When I first looked at this list, I couldn't help but wonder whether it's a teacher's fault when a student has these emotions and behaviors. I kept going back and forth: maybe it is, maybe it's not. After a while I concluded that assigning blame is irrelevant. The important thing for any teacher is to notice these emotions and behaviors, discern what might help the student, and implement that solution or as many solutions as it takes to address the problem. As all of us know, not every problem can be solved. But if there is pain, one can try to relieve it, and the simple attempt at relieving pain has merit. It's good practice to find pain and try to relieve it whether one is successful or not.

Once I had a class in which two students dominated every discussion. The other students were angry that those two were ruling every discussion. The quieter students had begun to sigh audibly when one of the dominating students raised his or her hand. I tried calling on students who didn't have their hands raised, I had the class work in groups, I used a lot of techniques to bring balance, but none worked for long.[14] Finally I tried a more overt approach. I brought in a series of cards on which I had written phrases such as "Must talk three times" and "Can only talk two times." I explained that each student would receive either three or two cards depending on their self-categorization. Each time a person spoke, he or she was to throw one of the cards into the center of the room.

I then asked who thought they needed some help in limiting their contribution to take two "can only talk two times" cards. The two dominating students, laughing, did. When, immediately upon being handed the cards, one of these students burst out with a technical question, I walked over and, smiling, threw one of his two "can only talk two times" cards into the center of the room. (Yes, he was frustrated. Yes, I was nervous. But after all, the whole point of the game was to help him and the other be quiet so others could speak. I checked in with him after class to make sure he was not hurt by the event. He was frustrated but not alienated. He understood the reasons behind my actions.) The game didn't solve the problem, and if we hadn't enjoyed the rapport that we did, it could have backfired and caused pain. We did enjoy that rapport, however, and the game did help. It made public and obvious a problem we were all aware of and frustrated by. We all wanted to solve the problem but were stymied by it. At the very least the game allowed us to address publicly what the quieter students were angry about (number one above), what the "domineering" students were troubled by (number two above). Both groups had perceptual problems (numbers five and six) that were addressed by the structure of the game. Students dominating a class often come to believe that the class would have no discussion at all were they not there to bear the burden. It's a skewed perception, but one can see how they get it—the other students just don't seem to want to talk and become less and less participatory as the weeks pass. Finally the talking students conclude that their talking is a service to the community, and the community would be lost without it. Similarly, the quieter students can come to blame the more talkative ones. If those others would just be quiet, they think, we could all have a real discussion that included everyone. Because the cards both limited the speech of the talkative students and put responsibility on the quieter ones to speak more often, the game demonstrated a more accurate and complex perception of the situation: everyone had power and responsibility to create the class discussion and doing this was not as easy as we might like.

Letting Bygones Be Bygones: The Advantages of "Covering over with Grass"

Sometimes a disagreement comes to the point when everyone involved has done a number of disrespectful things, large and

small. According to the Buddhist texts, the large ones (those calling for serious censure or when a monk "reviles and dispar-
ages"[15] the laity) must be addressed carefully, of course, but what
of the small ones? Once things had become messy in this way, the
Buddha recommended a technique called "covering over with
grass"—as in, throwing grass over a pile of excrement to remove
the bad smell.[16] Simply put, a representative from each side of
the dispute stands up and asks permission to let these smaller
problems be put aside. In the modern classroom a teacher can
easily instigate this sort of dispute management, but students
need guidance in two main ways: (1) to see the value of
letting-go, and (2) to perceive clearly (really: to feel) how small
what they are being asked to let go (or sacrifice) is. The best way
to handle this includes asking students to name the advantages
and make a list on the board. As to the clear perception of the
small size of the sacrifice, a teacher can invite the student who
seems most troubled to argue for the low value of what is being
let go. Such a practice forces the student to adopt a point of view
not his own—a good stretch, and he may convince himself that
the sacrifice is small. After that student has done so, the teacher
can check in with that student—what is being covered with grass
might seem too malodorous for such easy treatment, and that
problem must be addressed.

The True Depths of Community

Because of conceptions of anattā (not-self), karma, and life, Buddhists generally view the world and our communities in both
broad and intimate fashions. In the Buddhist conception, all humans have been born previously as animals, hell-beings, hungry
ghosts, and deities. In the round of rebirth and suffering, we
have taken many forms over our lifetimes. This view implies that
we have played many different roles in many different situations. Ethics, then, are founded not on what makes each individual special and different and worthy of being cherished, but on
the vast experiences each one of us has from our past roles and
on the value of transforming our intentions so as to act out of
generosity, kindness, and understanding.[17] We have each of us
left a glass of water in a bathroom. We have each one of us taken

offense. We have each prematurely exonerated the leaver of the glass. We have all gossiped unhelpfully. Remembering this, we can better relate to any member of our classroom community. We have, after all, been each member of any community at some point in our travels in the round of rebirth and suffering.

CHAPTER 3

Stopping a Raging Elephant Dead in Its Tracks

Irritation, Anger, and Rage

A person given to cruelty has non-cruelty by which to avoid it.
—Majjhima Nikāya 8:14.1

Sometimes when filled with rage I react, lash out, yell, leave. Later, I angrily justify my actions in my mind or regret what I've said, what I've done. Damage, sometimes irreparable, has been done to others, to me, and to relationships because of a rage reaction. These reactions are rarely helpful. The *feeling* of rage, however, can clarify things. Rage can illuminate problems, areas of karmic concern, and injustices. With a light shone so dramatically, one can work with loving-kindness to solve problems, to give attention where it's evidently needed. Rage, then, in a Buddhist framework, is better seen as evidence calling for curiosity than as a state over which you have no control. To begin to understand how anger can be a call for curiosity in the classroom, let's look at teachers' anger.

As an undergraduate, I once took a class the main structure of which I did not understand—I didn't know why we were doing what when. But I enjoyed the lectures and books, and that's all there was to the class as far as I could tell, so I enjoyed what I thought was there and did my work. Occasionally I was much moved by one of the readings, but I knew no one else in the class and there was no discussion, just lecture, so I didn't get to know anyone and any emotions I had were isolated and seemed pretty irrelevant. The class was not a big deal for me; it wasn't one of

those classes that swept me away with it or one that left me enraged every day. It was just a class in which there were sometimes interesting readings and lectures. Sitting in chairs with
fold-down desks in an amphitheater classroom, we looked down
from our comfortable, padded seats at our professor standing in
his half-circle surrounded by blackboards.

One day that small, thin man, who had been lecturing to our
class three times a week for more than half the semester now,
walked in and had a tirade. He stormed and harangued and
paced and shook his finger at us. He ranted and yelled. I don't remember exactly what he said—it's been more than two
decades—but I remember he berated us for not arguing over aspects of the material, for just sitting there like lumps.

Of course I was angry right back at him. Who did he think I
was? He didn't know me. He had no idea who I was. Outside the
classroom I was an engaged, high energy, risk-taking person
who loved the intellectual life so much that I would stay up all
night reading just because I was too excited about the material to
stop. In the wee hours, in the dorm, I summarized complex theo-
ries on the white boards of my hallmates' doors. As the professor
went on and on, I thought about standing up and walking out. I
thought about indignantly gathering my books and striding
right out that door. I didn't, though, and neither did anyone else.
We sat there like lumps.

As I reflect on this incident so many years later, I wonder
what was going on with that professor and his perception of our
relationship. He thought we were lumps, and from his perspective, based on the data he had, we were. But everything about the
class *told* us to be lumps, at least when we were there. Our classroom design told us to sit and listen to him. His formatted lectures told us to sit and listen to him. So we sat and listened.

What should I have done? Walked out? Written a letter explaining? Answered back? Now, at age 44, I have a lot of choices
about how to respond to that situation, but then I had only a tiny
repertoire of possible responses. The incident hit an artery for
me, and not just because I had never before seen a college professor enraged like that. I was wounded because someone I didn't
know assumed wrongly that he knew me and, based on that er-
roneous assumption, judged me harshly. Here's one of my dream
answers. I would stand up from where I sat in the class. I would

say, "I am sorry you have so many negative emotions about our class, but you have made many assumptions about us while you know nothing about us. Nor have you tried to learn about us. I think your negative emotions are a response to your isolation and have little to do with us and our relationship to the material of the class."

That answer gives me a satisfying, righteous sort of feeling, but a better way to address it would probably be a straighter line through empathy and curiosity—instead of righteousness. I could ask to see him in his office and tell him, "I am sorry you are angry. What can we do to help?" A bit patronizing, yes, but after all he had just thrown a tantrum. At least that way I would have been exploring what was going on with the professor. We would have made ourselves into a team for learning.

About five years ago I had my own opportunity to stand in front of my class, red-faced and shaking with anger. The class had been going well—we had read two books together and had had vibrant conversations. On the day I got so angry, we were supposed to discuss the first half of the third book. I had prepared a series of exercises based on the reading. Right before the class began, a student stopped by my office and apologized for not doing the reading—there had been no more copies of the book at the bookstore. I wondered what had happened and how big the problem was. Had the bookstore bought too few books? How many students were in her position? How many would have remembered or looked again at the first page of the syllabus to note that I always put all the books we're reading in the library on reserve in case something like this happened or in case a student couldn't afford to buy the books?

I walked into the classroom. I took roll. I looked at my students. I said, "I understand there was some difficulty getting ahold of the book required for today. Who was able to do the reading?"

Susan, the only sophomore in a class of juniors and seniors, raised her hand.

I was a violent storm, stopped dead in front of those students trying to regain my composure. I wanted to throw my files and books on the floor and storm out. I wanted to break something. I could feel adrenaline shooting through my veins. I thought, "Only *one* student? And that student a *sophomore*? What are we teaching these students to do here anyway? Are we just training them in passivity?" I remembered that teacher's rage from so long ago, and I remembered how we had sat so still in response. I remembered also that the reason I had been with those others in that classroom was to learn, and I remembered that the reason I was in this classroom now was to help others learn. Had the silence and compliance in that classroom so long ago indicated anything about learning? Maybe not. Maybe it reflected the quality of our relationship with the teacher right then: bad. By yelling, that teacher had simply increased our fear, stress, and defensiveness, and we had responded with silence.[1] I struggled not to yell. A stillness filled the room. I took a breath and said to Susan and the class, talking aloud to myself, almost in a fugue state: "I am not sure what to do. I am very angry. But should I cancel class? The book is on reserve at the library, as per the first page of your syllabus. Everyone in this classroom could have done the reading. Yet how many of you remembered that? How many of you decided to reread the syllabus because you couldn't buy the book? Why would you have done that?"

I knew that had each student known, the night before, by around 7 p.m., that every other student had been unable to buy the book and do the reading, someone probably would have called me and told me. Most of these students belonged to a certain demographic group and had certain values, and one of the twenty would have taken on that leadership role had he or she known the full story. But every student didn't know that story. This was a bunch of individuals, and each had independently learned a part of the problem and had reacted to the situation with pretty standard behavior. At age 20 I think I would have done exactly the same thing that most of them had done—run into a problem with the reading and not given another thought to the other students or the class as a whole. I would have assumed I was the only one with the problem, and I would have decided (if "decided" is really the word for such an easy mental acquiescence) to coast that day on the work of others. It wasn't my fault the bookstore didn't have the book, and others would have done the reading.

In the end, Susan and I began a dialogue—we worked through the exercises that I had prepared for the class in a way, only through a dialogue. As we focused on the material, I calmed down. Eventually others in the class joined in and a real discussion occurred, a discussion in which students were engaged and learning.

Most students ended that class, I think, having witnessed me extremely angry and having learned something despite their not doing the reading and despite my huge, nearly debilitating anger. But I am not at all sure that I handled that well. We made the best of things. And Susan did a superb job carrying the class. I'm not certain, however, we learned that day what we needed to learn, what the karmic setup was for.

What do I mean, karmic setup? From a Buddhist perspective, our intentional actions in the past form our view of the world, our situation, our physical, intellectual, and character attributes. Often ingrained through repetitious behavior, these views, situations, and attributes leave us more closed to some possibilities and more open to others. For example, suppose every Friday night you fix yourself a particular meal and watch a particular TV program. Suppose every Friday night another person volunteers at the snack counter at the school game. Come a Friday night, you are more likely to be fixing yourself a meal while the other person is more likely to be serving food to others. You *can* volunteer at the snack counter; you're just less likely to because that's not what you've practiced doing. We can deepen the example easily. Suppose when a student sarcastically rolls her eyes at you, you roll your eyes back and make a cutting, sarcastic comment. From a Buddhist view, you are practicing rolling your eyes and making sarcastic comments. You are habituating nasty emotions (anger, somewhat disguised, in my view) and rude behavior. Because you've taken an opportunity to practice these things, you are more likely to be nasty, sarcastic, and rude in the future.

Your intentional actions, thoughts, and speech in the past have helped create your situation, your view of the situation, and your likely response to that situation. But, and this is an aspect of karmic theory that even Buddhists often misunderstand, the liberating aspect of karmic theory is this: that while karmic results determine your situation and your likely response, they don't determine your response. At every single moment, blinded by anger, fear, or desire, you can choose to pause and cultivate loving-kindness, compassion, generosity, clarity, and understanding. Each moment you choose to cultivate these qualities, you ingrain a new habitual response. A driver cuts you off and just as you begin muttering to yourself you catch yourself and decide to wish him well: "May that driver arrive home safely."

The next time a driver does something vexing, you are more likely now to wish him well. This isn't easy. I find it difficult just to read the Buddhist texts explaining this. One such text just has a long list of bad qualities and their opposites. The text assures the reader or listener that the beauty of things like anger, greed, and delusion, is that their presence assures us of the possibilities of loving-kindness, generosity, clarity, and understanding. That means when you feel rage at the rudeness of others, you can be glad of the possibility of loving them. Really exasperating. A little difficult in the face of, for example, all your students coming to class unprepared. Here are parts of what the text says:

> A person given to cruelty has non-cruelty by which to avoid it.
> One given to killing living beings has abstention from killing living beings by which to avoid it. . . .
> One given to ill will has non-ill will by which to avoid it. . .
> One given to anger has non-anger by which to avoid it.
> One given to revenge has non-revenge by which to avoid it.
> One given to contempt has non-contempt by which to avoid it.
> One given to a domineering attitude has a non-domineering attitude by which to avoid it.[2]

Maddening though this list is, it makes a critical point about liberation. The triumvirate of Buddhist practice—meditation, ethics, and wisdom—together create greater possibility of helpful response. Instead of getting hit and so automatically hitting back, I can step back and look at the suffering in the situation and find that it's not just mine and in fact, it's not really mine at all. Everyone is suffering in some way and realizing that helps me abandon negative thoughts that spin in my head: planning retribution or reliving the pain. Rather, I can move on and help relieve the suffering. After all, if karmic theory is right, justice and retribution are already taken care of. I don't have to be in charge of justice or retribution; it's going to happen no matter what I do. (Even if karmic theory is wrong, would I rather have my mind filled with plans for revenge or plans to treat others with kindness? Revenge plans are stimulating, but they're not pleasant in the long run.) This lack of responsibility for justice, however, doesn't mean I don't have responsibilities. I am in charge of loving-kindness and compassion.

Eventually when someone cuts you off or does something irritating you might even find yourself not being annoyed at all. Rather, the incident has become simply a cue to wish another well. (Consider what a teacher can do when a student rolls her eyes at him. Queryingly raise his eyebrows? With real curiosity, ask her what's up?)

I want to pause here and point something out about view. Note that I said past intentional actions, thoughts, and speech have helped create your situation, *your view of the situation*, and your likely response. So when I say the Friday night TV-watcher is less likely to think of volunteering at a snack counter as an option, I mean that her view of Friday nights is somewhat limited. Not only that, but the TV-watcher is more likely to be thinking of whether or not what's on TV is to her taste. Her perspective, what she thinks about, has been formed by her habits. She does not think of Friday nights as a time to extend generosity toward others. From a Buddhist perspective, that's a limited view. Just as a view that a driver who cuts you off is a cause of irritation is limited compared to a view that invites the same stimulus to offer a moment of joy at being cued to wish that person well.

One time a man let loose a savage elephant with a reputation for killing humans to attack the Buddha. The elephant raised his trunk and charged the Buddha at full speed. Though his monks warned him and advised him to move out of the elephant's path, the Buddha refused. He claimed that no one can take an enlightened person's life by violence. Standing in front of the charging elephant, the Buddha sent it thoughts of loving-kindness. The elephant slowed, lowered his trunk, and then stood before the Buddha, allowing the Buddha to stroke his forehead. The elephant then took dust from the feet of the Buddha and sprinkled it on his own head (symbolizing the elephant's respect—the dirt from the lowest part of the Buddha, his feet, was higher than the highest part of the elephant, its head) and finally retreated backwards until the Buddha was out of sight. In this way, that fierce elephant was tamed.[3] This story illustrates to me not only the power of loving-kindness but the predictability of anger. Anger is so often answered with anger that to answer it with something else is surprising.

In Buddhist theory and stories, the answer to rage is loving-kindness.

Meditation in particular opens a space between the feeling (when almost an entire class had not done the reading, of rage) and the response; instead of being defeated by fury, you now have the space in which to view it as a clue, a helpful indication, a reason for investigation. With the opening of a space, one has a growing awareness of the arrival of wrath. You can be aware of your heart beating faster, your blood pressure going up, your face flushing, your movements becoming jerky. You can watch the speed of your thoughts increase and become negative, barbed, attacking, dismissive. You can see your eagerness to spit words out. And, aware of these symptoms of rage, you have the space you need to choose a response—to take a deep breath and let it out, for example, to let go of those spinning thoughts. This space allows you to let the rage-filled part of you die, at least for a minute. Watching your symptoms of anger allows you to let the emotion die again, moment by moment.

With more meditation and more meditation in particular on loving-kindness, you can have greater equanimity in the classroom and fewer regrets about words, actions, and thoughts that are merely reactive to a given stimulus. Further, because of your periods of greater calm, you can perceive more of what's around you. When you view the world in two tones, black or white, for you or against you, you cause yourself either anger or pleasure. By limiting your view this way, you miss much of the beauty of the world. With meditation, on the other hand, you allow any number of emotions to color your world. You haven't sentenced yourself to a life informed by only a few emotions, so your emotional palette broadens. Further, your own complicity in whatever situation you're in becomes clearer. For example, it's easier now for me to have a more informed and nuanced perspective on Susan's success and the other students' and my failure in relation to the problem with that book. Susan had been prepared because she was excited about the class, vibrantly interested. She had fought to get into the class, and she had something to prove, being the only sophomore.

There were other factors, too. I'll give you two of the most influential: one, she had had me as a professor before—not only did that mean she had more personal allegiance to me, it also meant she remembered the books would be on reserve at the library. Further it meant she was more aware of my expectations and then, in class, was more comfortable talking with me. (Later, *after* class, giving me a chance to view my rage once again, two students came up and said they *had* been able to do the reading too because they had bought the books over the internet. They had been too intimidated by my large emotions, however, to admit to this during class, just as I, more than two decades before, had been too cowed by my own professor's rage to say anything.) Two, she was underloading that semester, taking three classes instead of four. In short, she had the motivation, the knowledge, the time, and the calm to do an excellent job. And, incidentally, she was very humble about all this—she told me about these two factors as a way for me to understand that any student in her situation would have done the same, that she wasn't special, just her circumstances were.

Let's look back at the books-on-reserve factor. Had I really *taught* the students that the books would be on reserve? Clearly they had not learned it: when the information became important, they did not remember and act on that information. All I had done was write it on the syllabus and then we had read that part of the syllabus aloud on the first day. So it turns out that that's not really teaching, though it allows me to say, "I told you so" (if I want to practice righteous smugness).

I know some colleagues who, in this sort of circumstance, walk out of their classes. If no one does the reading, they shame the students. I don't think I've ever done this, but that doesn't mean I am against it. I worry that I would do it in anger, frustration, and a simple desire to escape my suffering. If I could do it motivated by love, and it would help students, I'd do it.[4] After all, class time is precious. To flush any of it away is sacrilegious, and that's exactly what those other professors are communicating when they simply walk out of their classes upon discovering not enough students have done the reading—that the time is too important to be frittered away because of lack of preparation.

Buddhist theory and practice offers much on how to deal with anger in ways that lessen anger in the future. But other ways of preventing anger have to do with motivating students. How, for example, do I encourage students to keep up with the reading and other class-related outside-class work? I encourage, remind, invite reflection. In my 100-level classes I often pass around a little white card and as it goes around all the students write the page number they're on somewhere on the card—anonymously. I then tally up how many people are where on the board and give the students a progress report. It's good for the ones who are behind to see that their being behind is not normal, it doesn't reflect the general status of the class.[5]

This generalization—that because one student isn't doing the work he or she assumes others aren't either—has a huge impact on that student's experience of the class. We all get stuck in our own viewpoints, and from there we often cannot see other viewpoints. I know many students (myself included) who, if they miss class, believe that nothing much has happened. They weren't there to experience what happened and they have reason to want nothing to have happened. That way they haven't missed anything. So, consciously or not, they think nothing has happened. Or that nothing important has happened. (Certainly one of the most irritating but oft-repeated questions a teacher gets asked by students who have been absent is, "Did I miss anything important?")[6] Students who have not kept up with outside-class work often make similar assumptions. They believe at some level they would not learn anything from the reading even if they did it. And if they can find one student who shares their predicament or who doesn't object to their view, they are that much more reinforced in it. They're trapped by their own viewpoint. To counteract this strong self-deluding force, I occasionally invite students to reflect out loud about how they feel in general during class when they come unprepared. Safe to remember their feelings without shame (they volunteer to speak on this topic when I ask, and I suspect those who have not done the reading for that day are less likely to answer it), they remember with regret their feelings of ignorance, stupidity, and alienation. This public recognition educates and reminds others—they learn from the experience of peers, which has greater impact than any chiding from me.

I use a variety of techniques to help students keep up with class work. I call them at home. Not only individuals, but entire classes. I'm in a rare position of being able to autodial most of my students. If we're going through some particularly challenging times, I leave my students messages of encouragement. I share a joke we had in class. I try to be brief. More often than I'd like, I make a mistake on the syllabus or in something I said in class, so

I use these voicemail lists to correct those problems and also to encourage students.

Students often don't do their reading because they haven't gotten enough sleep, and teachers often trivialize the challenge of getting enough sleep. Look, however, at what students—at least college students—are doing: many come from a home environment to which they've had years to become accustomed that includes adults who, knowing the importance of sleep and having bodies less able to do without sleep, go to bed at a reasonable time. Suddenly students, who are able to get away with a lot with their young bodies, live in environments made up almost totally of people their age. They are all able to push physical limits a lot. Further, by the time most adults are forty, their social growth is quite different. But for young adults such as my students, forming social alliances is, because of their stage of development, one of the most important aspects of their lives. Now they live in a building in which they can make alliances twenty-four hours a day. In the first or second week of my lower level classes I give out a handout on sleep deprivation that outlines why and how to get enough sleep. (See Appendix II: Handouts for a copy.) I am on the verge of getting earplugs for them. Living with 50 other 20-year-olds in close contact wreaks havoc on sleep. It may not be my business how much they sleep, but I am their teacher. I am there to help them learn and learn how to learn. Sleep deprivation makes you less able to learn—it makes you stupid and depressed.[7] One researcher claims it's the single best determiner of performance—way beyond genes or environmental factors.

These techniques communicate to students what I expect of them. Students, knowing these expectations and knowing they'll be rewarded for meeting them—they'll have dynamic conversations in class, for example—respond, leading to better classes for me and fewer attacks of rage from feelings of helplessness and frustration.

Filling your teaching toolbox with a wide variety of tools makes teaching more fun and creative. You can pull out your staple gun when you want to connect something and your tape measure when you need to know something's length. It's also important, however, to accept that you'll have problems. You can't prevent every single problem you've ever had from ever occurring again. I've seen syllabi that have so many prohibitions they read more like a history of professional irritations than maps for a good class. The fact is that we will face many annoyances and some of them we will face again and again—that's the nature of our work. As Gilbert Highet points out:

> It is easy to like the young because they are young. They have no faults, except the very ones which they are asking you to eradicate: ignorance, shallowness, and inexperience. The really hateful faults are those which we grown men and women have. Some of these grow on us like diseases, others we build up and cherish as though they were virtues. Ingrained conceit, calculated cruelty, deep-rooted cowardice, slobbering greed, vulgar self-satisfaction, puffy laziness of mind and body—these and the other real sins result from years, decades of careful cultivation. They show on our faces, they ring harsh or hollow in our voices, they have become bone of our bone and flesh of our flesh. The young do not sin in those ways. Heaven knows they are infuriatingly lazy and unbelievably stupid and sometimes detestably cruel—but not for long, not all at once, and not (like grown-ups) as a matter of habit or policy. They are trying to be energetic and wise and kind. When you remember this, it is difficult not to like them.[8]

Because of the profession I've chosen, I will spend decades of my life in the company of young people who lack knowledge and experience. That's why they're spending time with me. Part of my work, then, is to gain experience and insight while avoiding careful cultivation of "ingrained conceit, calculated cruelty, deep-rooted cowardices" and the like. In a Buddhist framework, these qualities fall under the category of anger. Anger can range from mild distaste for the color of someone's shirt (so mild you don't even notice it but simply tend not to introduce yourself to that person at a gathering, for example) to the kind of crippling wrath that takes over a person's mind so she can think of nothing else. Anger encompasses disappointment, fear, guilt, anxiety, and despair. All these kinds of anger are to be answered with loving-kindness, no matter if the anger is directed toward one's self or others. With loving-kindness sufficiently developed, anyone can use it to stop a rampaging elephant or, in any classroom, on any day, to teach.

CHAPTER 4

Do Not Cross Line

Wonder and Imaginative Engagement

*Thus at that moment, at that instant, at that second, the cry spread as far as the
brahma world (celestial world), and this ten thousandfold world system shook,
quaked, and trembled, and an immeasurable glorious radiance appeared in the world
surpassing the divine majesty of the devas (celestial beings).*
—*Saṃyutta Nikāya* 56:11.1

When the Buddha gave his first teaching after his enlightenment,
Kondañña was the first person to understand. Kondañña's
"gaining of the Dhamma-eye" or "glimpse of nirvana" was the
climax of the Buddha's sermon. As soon as Kondañña had
understood, the exultant message was rapidly transmitted up
through various levels of gods: "The supreme Dhamma-wheel
had been set in motion by the 'Lord,' and could not be stopped
by any power."[1] In fact after celebrations in level after level of
deities, the entire "world system shook, quaked, and trembled,
and an immeasurable glorious radiance appeared in the world
surpassing the divine majesty of deities." The Buddha then exclaimed, "Kondañña has indeed understood! Kondañña has
indeed understood!" and Kondañña got a new name: Anna
Kondañña—Kondañña Who Has Understood.[2]

Imagine for just a moment what would have happened had a
similar fanfare occurred when the first student you ever taught
understood what you were teaching. Imagine that first student
really 'getting' algorithms as the building blocks of computer
programming. Or 'getting' the depths of reverberation of Greek
myths found in modern literature. Or 'getting' the complex bio-
logical ramifications of whether something can move away from

danger (a tree can't; a squirrel can). Imagine the first student in the first calculus class you ever taught having that moment of blissful understanding.

Imagine if the significance of that moment were so important that deities were alerted to the dawning of a new age—one that would be informed by what you taught. What if the whole world trembled and the student gained a new name? These days we don't even mildly celebrate understanding—whether it's of a theory that unlocks a single book or one that reveals the whole foundation of a type of literature. Never mind if the understanding signals the end of both a student's pain and her contribution to the pain of others—as, according to a Buddhist understanding, was Kondañña's moment—a moment informed only by generosity, loving-kindness, clarity, and understanding. A moment of wonder, in this context, is a physical, emotional, intellectual experience[3] of learning—a moment of insight into the truth of what is being taught.

Some of my most pleasurable memories from college are when I struggled with an exceedingly difficult text, and then, with a new level of understanding achieved, found there was nothing left to struggle with. After hours or days or even weeks of work, the meaning of the text suddenly became utterly clear. It felt as though the text had reached out, grabbed me by the front of my shirt, thrown me out the window, and left me panting on the sidewalk wondering where I was. Often after such a moment I would go to class and wonder if anyone else had experienced what I had. If so, how were their lives changing as a result? It felt odd to have such huge emotional responses in my private experience of what was, after all, a group involvement. It felt odd to keep those experiences private as though they were dirty little secrets. Yet on the few occasions when I did share such feelings, I was perceived as a brown noser, a geek, or just plain weird. Even my professors sometimes seemed confused by my actually having been moved by a text. But surely they, too, felt the beauty of the texts? Surely that's why they taught them? Describing students, Lillian Weber said, "They begin school an exclamation point and a question mark; too often they leave as a plain period."[4] I learned not to share my enthusiasm for a text in any context besides a one-on-one conversation in the professor's office, and often not even then.[5] Now that I'm a professor and have a bit more power in setting the classroom tone, I want to honor that feeling of being assaulted by a text and the intellectual piecing-together that follows it. I want to recognize publicly and explore the impact of what we're learning. At the very least, I can honor in my classroom a moment of experience that is filled with something like wonder as I similarly invite acknowledgment of negative feelings towards a text.[6] Some of the readings I assign for my classes, therefore, are not chosen because of their ability to help my students know facts, accumulate skills, or use methodologies, though they often do that, as well. I choose them, rather, because of their likelihood to grab my students by the fronts of their shirts and demand a complete restructuring of their worldviews. I select them because they force students to ask, "Where am I now and what must I do now that everything is changed?" If I know a homework assignment is likely to have left students breathless, I take a few moments at the beginning of class for comments on why those who loved the work loved it. And when, as a class, we dig into the text for facts, skills, or methodologies, I remind them of the value of awe. To move on to analysis too quickly is to ignore the beauty of the text itself and to devalue awe. Of course, analysis can often help us gain an even deeper appreciation of a text's beauty. It's one way to express at least respect for a text if not awe. But teachers and students can forget the value of awe too easily if we are too goal-oriented, if we pay too much attention to checking things off our lists in a timely fashion.

Part of awe is mystery, of course, and I fairly frequently have the class—myself included—do things the reasons for which are, well, mysterious at the outset. Sometimes I don't know the reasons at all, but I have an inclination to do something, to explore something, with students. I have learned to act on these inclinations, and I have learned that often afterward some of the reasons for our approach become clear. Students look at me wide-eyed and say, "Now I know why we did this!" and proceed to tell me.

Take, for example, the Council of All Beings. In this exercise, each participant becomes a non-human being (an animal, a plant, a feature of nature) and speaks from the perspective of that being in a council meeting.[7] Each being or aspect of nature has a chance to speak. Ideally the Council is done in a multi-day workshop for people interested in sustainability issues, and people are given time in an afternoon or evening to relax and allow a being or aspect of nature to choose them as they take a walk outside. Participants often make masks that allow them to feel their new role more deeply and to speak for the being or aspect of nature clearly. The next day all gather in a circle with their masks on, and the facilitator calls the formal council to order. A meeting of animals, plants, and features of nature begins. Each being is invited to speak for itself and for nature, to air their troubles.

Only nonhumans speak. The council excludes or marginalizes humans. After all, human beings get to talk all the time, and it's their actions that have made victims of so many, including themselves. At some councils, there are no "humans" at the meeting. At other councils, designated humans listen as part of the circle; at others, they sit in the middle of the circle to better hear the voices of the non-humans.

After every being has spoken, a number of different things can happen. For example, should the humans be present and perhaps showing their suffering (it's hard to listen so directly and publicly to the ways humans have hurt non-humans), a few beings might offer the specific strengths they have to the humans as humans work to solve the problems.

The first time I held such a council in class, I was not sure why we should do it or what it might result in. I told my students that I had two plans for the class—one was a traditional discussion of our reading, the other was this council. They got to choose. The students murmured a bit and then one said (it was about midway through the semester), "I don't know about you, but all my classes today have been so boring, I'm willing to give this a try just because it's *different*." That comment carried the day.

What did the students and I gain from the exercise? For a long while I wasn't sure. As a fellow professor who was familiar with the exercise said, "It's *cool*, definitely. But what do we *learn*?"[8] Having led such a council twice now and having discussed it with a lot of people, I can explain a few outcomes. First, each participant connects more intimately with fellow council members. Learning what being chose someone or which being someone chose and how they speak as that being allows everyone present to know a very different part of that person, a part that is often silent and silenced in normal discussions. This kind of acquaintance with another and the acceptance practiced as one listens creates intimacy—a closeness. This closeness can be a fine foundation for moral sensitivity and intellectual clarity. And since I see precious little in our formal education about intimacy and took a long time to learn some of its key aspects myself, I particularly welcome that aspect of the council.

Participants, however, experience and learn more than that. They are introduced to aspects of the environment in such a personal way that these aspects now become more real and important to them. (Participants don't research their being, though I suppose they could. Rather, they depend on what they already know intellectually but haven't known in this more emotional way.) I had never seen a Douglas Fir before I heard a student speak as one. When I later saw a Douglas Fir, I not only knew a bit about the tree and the environmental dangers it faces but I knew a bit about it from a student to whom I now felt personally connected. It's as though that knowledge had a personal tag on it, so the tree was more important to me in complex ways.

The creators of the Council describe its purpose this way: "It is excellent for growing the ecological self, for it brings a sense of solidarity with all life, and fresh appreciation for the damage wrought by one upstart species."9 Yes and no. Yes, it cultivates a sense of solidarity with different beings and aspects of nature. Yes, it brings greater knowledge of specific problems humans have created. But this understanding of negative human impact does more—it puts in relief one of the most difficult aspects of being concerned about the environment: We created the problem. We are guilty. Will I ever forget the student who spoke as acid rain? Her mask was more of a talisman—a smokestack made of paper with smoke coming out of the top and a large black drop of water at its side. She accused humans of stealing her life-giving quality as water and transforming her into poison. In our discussion afterward we learned why her statement resonated so strongly for us. She had captured what we felt as humans in our oil-dependent, polluting age: that our life-giving had somehow been distorted into death-making. By emphasizing our culpability, the council allows us to face the most emotional part of the environmental problems, the part that can paralyze people or make them stubbornly dismissive. The exercise allows us to be non-human long enough to feel the tension of contributing to all the problems and responding them as well—of being solidly in the web of nature, neither all good nor all bad.

None of these reasons, however, was the reason why I held my first council in class. I held the first council because it was an interesting possibility. It looked as if something like learning might happen. I was curious.

Another way to respect wonder in the classroom is by using guided imagery, which I used for the first time when I led the Council. Because of the time restraints, I couldn't allow the students to walk around outside and relax until they knew intuitively what being or aspect of nature they should be. (The directions in Macy and Brown's book specify that in the best circumstances, the being chooses the participant.) So I designed a guided meditation for the students on the spot. I told them to close their eyes, relax, and imagine themselves in a certain situation. I led them in a ten-minute guided imagery exercise that allowed a particular being to come to mind. I could design such a meditation quickly because of my own experience with the kinds of visualizations encouraged in different Buddhist traditions. Simple practices include meditating in front of a colored disk until one can make that disk appear in one's mind at will and then mentally manipulate the disk in other ways. Some Buddhist practices include complex visualizations. In Tibetan tantric deity yoga, for example, the practitioner systematically visualizes a particular deity in great detail so that the deity becomes as real to the practitioner as any human being. As with the simpler meditation on the disks, the meditator can now call the deity to mind at will in all its detail and with all its strengths. Thus the practitioner becomes directly aware of a deity and its strengths and is able to share in those qualities.[10]

After our Council, students commented on the value of the guided meditation that prepared them for it. Most said they'd never done such a thing before. It seemed to open a part of them that was often closed in class, and it fostered an ease in creativity. They were right. They were learning another way of thinking. Guided imagery—a scheduled time during which one cultivates a relaxed, receptive state and experiences, through one's imagination, something not immediately present at the moment—is not just for relaxation or entertainment. It can be a useful tool for learning, as well.[11]

In *Teaching for the Two-Sided Mind: A Guide to Right Brain/Left Brain Education,* Linda Verlee Williams explores the importance of students gaining an understanding of the use of their imaginations and how to control their imaginations. She writes that guided imagery is a good way to introduce new material to a class and to review material. She even suggests using guided imagery to help students engage in writing activities and shows how teachers can grade this kind of learning. My own imagination runs wild. Could psychology students learning about mental illnesses imagine themselves similarly ill and thus not only review the specifics of those illnesses but also cultivate empathy and compassion for its sufferers? Better yet, could students of psychology imagine what mental health truly feels like and aspire to achieve it and discern its various obstacles? Could a literature teacher lead a class in guided imagery to reveal to students complexities implied but not overt in a text? —complexities of character and motivation that could deepen the exploration of a text?[12] Williams discusses guided imagery on botanical functions; students review the parts of a plant as they are guided through that plant. Could students do a guided imagery in physics and somehow explore different subatomic particles? Guided imagery in this way functions as a review of the material with greater personalization of it. That means better recall, studies show. Whether used to introduce material or review material, it can cultivate imagination—that used to create great literature, to design scientific experiments, and to envision ourselves into a better world.

I am fascinated by how the imagination works and how to help students learn how to control their imaginations. One aspect of Williams' discussion of guided imagery brought me up short, however. She warns teachers "to consider the effects a fantasy is likely to have on students." Because fantasies evoke such personal images, it's hard to predict student responses. Williams writes that while "a birth fantasy may seem harmless to you, [it] could have a devastating effect on a girl who's had an abortion." She warns that teachers must use guided imagery with sensitivity. She suggests using only positive imagery and avoiding emotionally charged subjects in order to prevent problems. Further, she cautions teachers to be "sensitive to students' reactions during and after the fantasy."[13]

I was struck by the paragraph. Of course, yes, one needs to be careful and sensitive and responsive as often as one can, including when one does guided imagery. But are our students' minds so dangerous that they should be wrapped with bright orange "Do Not Cross" tape? Have we given our young so little guidance in the use of their minds that we need to consult psychologists when we bring up a topic in a certain way?

Regrettably I have to reply with a yes, and two points follow from that: (1) Because our students are culturally disadvantaged at using their minds these ways, we are all the more responsible to help them learn how. Students routinely underestimate the powers of their own minds. (For example, when heart rate monitors first became readily available to the public I bought one for cycling training and was amused at parties to hand the readout instrument to others and let them watch as I raised and lowered my heart beat at will. Decades later students are still astonished that I can do this, but anyone can learn to do this in less than three minutes.) (2) Bringing these sorts of experiments and practices into the classroom is going to bring you trouble. Even leading students in simple deep breathing alone (often done as part of the preparation for guided imagery), can cause problems. This kind of exercise "was eliminated from the proposed health curriculum in Michigan after public concern that it could encourage devil worship and mysticism." A bill was brought before the South Carolina House in 1992 to similarly outlaw breathing and attention exercises from public schools. (Fortunately, it was defeated.)[14] Knowing these sorts of practices are valuable while likely to bring you calamity is, of course, all the more reason to include these sorts of exercises in the classroom, give students choices about participating, and encourage open discussion of the issues. As to accepting difficulties, I try to avoid trouble about trivial things and walk into mine fields only for important issues. I try to remember that attempting to avoid all complications and difficulties won't make me teach any better.

I have rarely been challenged for using guided imagery and other creative exercises of the mind, and most often challenges come only in indirect ways, such as on the occasional anonymous student evaluation. These challenges are good reasons to include them—to help my students see the powers and strengths of their minds so they can use it effectively, not fear and avoid it.

Two of my own teachers beautifully took in stride the wonders of the mind. I was prone to hallucinations or visions when I was younger.[15] Once, quite nervous about these experiences and concerned for my sanity, I mentioned having a series of hallucinations to one of my professors. My underlying question was: Am I insane? Does it mean you're insane if you see things others don't see? My professor smiled appreciatively and told me Jean Paul Sartre had had hallucinations of a large blue crab for months. I thought, "Jean Paul Sartre?! My hero?! Then it must be OK to have hallucinations." I found that accepting them as my professor had, as one of the things minds do, rather than as symptoms of disease, allowed me to have them with considerably less anxiety. By the time I met Sister Khema in Sri Lanka, I had more or less accepted the visions as part of my life. So when I told her of the visions I was having of deities all about the island, I was testing her. (Looking back on it, testing Ayya Khema was a big part of my time with her.) What would she say about them? Instead of telling me anything directly, she asked me a question about them: "Do you find your work is lighter when they are there?" I looked at her as though she were the one with mental problems. Why would my work be lighter just because non-corporeal beings were around? My work at the nunnery was quite physical— I carried buckets of water for hours every day all over the island to feed the new plants. To give myself breaks from the heavy labor and to protect young plants from the tropical sun, I fashioned little hats for them out of huge, dry leaves. How could a few deities help? "No, why?" I replied. "Oh, you know," she said, turning away, "sometimes they help out."

One power of the mind is wonder. It's a power recognized by all the worlds when Kondañña understood the Buddha's teaching, a power celebrated by the Buddha himself when he exclaimed that "Kondañña has indeed understood!" The power of wonder can be cultivated through imaginative exercises such as the Council of All Beings and guided imagery. Even simple acceptance of the magnitude of mental experience is one way to honor it. Last semester I took a class on the works of William Faulkner that began at an awkward time—almost a full week after other classes had begun. Because the professor didn't want us to wait a week before we started reading, he e-mailed us an assignment for the first class. He wrote: "The first three stories along with 'That Evening Sun' are among the finest short stories in the English Language. Have fun."[16] Now *that's* the way to start a class. As I read the first story I thought, "This is the most amazing story I've ever read. How did Faulkner do this?" My wonder led to analysis.

That's a fine way to proceed. From wonder to analysis, naturally.

CHAPTER 5

Homicidal Tendencies

The Story of a Teacher and a Student

A blessing it is to refrain from doing wrongs.
—*Dhammapada* 333

In the time of the Buddha, a boy was born to a royal chaplain.[1] His parents were delighted, but troubled: their child was born in the robber constellation, and therefore inclined to commit ill deeds—he was astrologically disadvantaged. They worked hard to overcome this problem, educating their son well and naming him Ahiṁsaka, which means Harmless.

When he came of age, a fine teacher accepted Ahiṁsaka as his student. Ahiṁsaka prospered there, both in his studies and his humility. But prosperity breeds envy, and as Ahiṁsaka grew near to graduation, other students plotted against him. It wasn't easy, but in the end, they convinced the teacher that his favorite student was seeking to supplant him. To the teacher, the solution was clear: *Ahiṁsaka* must die.[2]

Now, the duty of any graduating student was to present his teacher with a gift, and in this ritual obligation the teacher saw his opportunity. He asked Ahiṁsaka to bring him 1000 fingers—human fingers. All of them must be little fingers from right hands, the teacher said. This, the teacher believed, would lead to Ahiṁsaka's arrest and a death sentence if he didn't die at the hands of those he attacked.

At first, Ahiṁsaka was horrified: cut the fingers from people's hands? But his teacher reminded him that if his learning didn't conclude with the proper ceremony, his years of study would be fruitless.

Ahiṁsaka left the teacher. Drawing on the inclinations his birth in the robber constellation had given him, he became a notorious killer. He collected the little fingers of his victims and strung them around his neck. Displayed in this hideous way, the fingers didn't decompose into dust and Ahiṁsaka didn't lose the proof they provided of his success. Thus he earned his new name: Aṅgulimāla, or "necklace of fingers." Nine hundred and ninety-nine fingers later, Aṅgulimāla had one kill left to make before he could present his beloved teacher with the required gruesome gift. Meanwhile, his parents knew nothing about their son. But the more she heard about this Aṅgulimāla, this necklace of fingers, the more convinced his mother became that it must be her son—and that she must find and help him.

The Buddha heard what was happening also and realized Aṅgulimāla's grave danger: would his one thousandth victim be his mother, guaranteeing him a place in hell for eons? And so the story brings us to its climax, when Aṅgulimāla, distracted from the sight of the woman approaching him (his mother, whom he doesn't recognize), runs after the Buddha, who has come to prevent him from killing her. Aṅgulimāla runs and runs after the Buddha, but the Buddha does not allow himself to be caught. Aṅgulimāla is awestruck and stops in his tracks. He has outrun some of the fastest beasts on earth, but he can't catch up to this simple renunciant, who, from all appearances, is idly strolling along.

Aṅgulimāla calls out, "Stop, recluse! Stop, recluse!"

The Buddha replies, "I have stopped, Aṅgulimāla. You stop, too."

Aṅgulimāla can't help but notice the inconsistency. In fact, it is Aṅgulimāla who has stopped and the Buddha who keeps on walking. He asks the Buddha what he means.

The Buddha replies: "I have stopped forever. I abstain from violence toward living beings, but you have no restraint toward things that breathe. So I have stopped and you have not."[3]

At the Buddha's words, everything changes for Aṅgulimāla. On the spot he throws away his weapons and vows to avoid violence. He worships at the Buddha's feet and asks that he be allowed to become a monk, a recluse, a follower of the Buddha.

***

What does this story of a serial killer have to do with teaching and learning? Of course it's not just what's in the text that's important here—it's the interpretations. And no single interpretation will ever be enough; any story, to be useful and rich, needs to be open for different interpretations over time and by different people. So what are the interpretations of the Aṅgulimāla story that have the most meaning to me as a teacher and learner these days?

In the simplest terms, what I take from this story is that every student and every teacher has the potential to do great harm to others. Everyone can act for ill out of fear and be misled and thus do serious harm. In fact, many of us spend a lot of time fearful and misled, and harming others because of our emotions and naiveté. In this way there are never good or bad teachers, never good or bad students. It's just not that clear. But there's transformation here, and hope. Hope through other people, hard work, happenstance, communication, wisdom, clarity, compassion. Because of the central tenet of Buddhist philosophy, paṭicca samuppāda, no unenlightened one can have a complete picture of what's going on, and no one (enlightened or not) is ever powerless. Being in the web of causes and effects, one not always *can* have an effect, one necessarily *does*.

If one ponders only the impressively quick transformation of Aṅgulimāla into a killer, one quickly concludes that he is trapped by karma: born into the robber constellation, Aṅgulimāla becomes a horrendous thief. In fact, though, Aṅgulimāla denies karmic fatalism two times: when, despite his astrological sign, he becomes a fine and loving student, and later, after becoming a mass murderer, when he transforms himself into a monk. So one of the strengths of the story is that it communicates moments of potential—moments that seem to portend a negative outcome are actually revealed to hold dynamic possibility of good. In fact this story is a quick answer to anyone's misinterpreting karma to be fatalistic. Aṅgulimāla, after all, killed 999 people. Surely he must spend eons in saṃsāra, suffering the karmic results of what he'd done.

But no. Most certainly not. In fact what might have partially inspired his seriousness in becoming a monk and vowing to become enlightened (which he did, later in that same life), was his knowledge that unless he became enlightened, unless he abandoned saṃsāra altogether, his suffering in the future in various saṁsaric realms would be beyond words. So pedagogically, those students (and teachers) who have the greatest challenges also may reap the greatest benefits from learning—they (we) are perhaps in the best position to experience and value the transformative power of education. My greatest teachers and mentors have clearly known this. For example, when I was a sophomore in Dr. Flynn's philosophy class, there was little to recommend me. My preparation for college had been poor, my discipline was undependable, my social skills were practically nonexistent. Yet his attention to my intellect through comments on my papers and discussions in his office allowed an unforeseeable transformation.

The story of Aṅgulimāla gives a dramatic example of the powers of learning, but the story gives more as more questions are asked of it. For example, where does the whole problem that comes to rule Aṅgulimāla's life begin? At birth. Whether or not you take astrological interpretations seriously (many Buddhists all over the world take them very seriously), we all begin with our specific contexts—a set of circumstances that define us from early on: who our parents are, what their relationship is, what socioeconomic class they're in, what race/ethnicity we are, where we're born and the problems specific to that area. And no matter what path we follow, the elements of that context have power over us that can show themselves at any and odd times.

Another root of Aṅgulimāla's problem is the envy of his fellow students, who, unable to experience altruistic joy, seek his downfall. He must also deal with the envy of his teacher—who wants to make sure his student does not exceed his own skills and reputation and so defeat him, and who then uses his power as a teacher and the student's duty to him to lead Aṅgulimāla astray.

For teachers, these roots reveal the importance of knowing our own birth contexts and certainly demand that we at least try to take into account the unique contexts of our students. Also the story warns us of the power of envy and the importance of cultivating altruistic joy. Really, what is success for a teacher but that his or her students work together, learning and teaching? And what is fruition if not the students' exceeding the teacher's own skills and reputation? What could better define a teacher's achievement but a student's greater success or better yet *many* students' greater accomplishments? Even quite recently, however, deeply hidden envy caused me to speak carelessly to a student. I

hardly knew her and had every reason to respect her drive and efforts, but a moment came when I was blinded by the advantages
she had over so many others and, yes, over what I had had. She
seemed oblivious to these advantages. I didn't condemn her; I
didn't yell at her. Rather, I righteously called her to mentor others
in the future—those who had had fewer advantages. Right
though I may have been to try to spur her sense of responsibility
to others, though, she heard my anger and was deeply angered
herself. More than a year later, the misunderstanding created an
even bigger mess, all because of my inability to cultivate deep altruistic joy. Similarly, Aṅgulimāla's teacher and the other students
lack both altruistic joy and, well, the opposite of fear. (But hold
on, because you may think that's courage. In Buddhism the opposite of fear, however, is loving-kindness. See chapter 3: Stopping a
Raging Elephant Dead in Its Tracks.)

This reading of the story, recognizing the powers of envy and
fear, leads us to what in Buddhism are called the four divine
abidings (brahma-vihāras). Loving-kindness (mettā), compassion (karunā), altruistic joy (muditā), and equanimity (upekkha)
are qualities that can be developed to make the mind "immeasurable." (So they are referred to as the "immeasurables").

All four are important, but altruistic joy is most relevant here.
This is delight in the happiness of others, the kind of elation you
can feel so naturally when you laugh with your child as that
child takes its first steps and seems to feel how significant and
delightful that is. But it's harder somehow to feel when your
friend gets a better education or job than you do or higher pay or
a more kind or beautiful partner. Or an education, job, money, or
partner at all. What is more natural to feel is jealousy or discon-
tent. Sometimes it's easier to take pleasure in, say, a lawyer
friend's having been made partner than a fellow teacher in your
department winning a teaching award. The closer the person is
to your area—personally, professionally, geographically, the
more difficult it is to feel altruistic joy.

But again, what is one kind of emotional success for a teacher
but joy in the joys of others, joy in the success of students? Self-
less joy? Students are smarter, have more advantages, get into
great schools, make loads of money. A teacher can delight in their
success, letting go of even the slightest twinge of envy.

Aṅgulimāla is known to Buddhists as a reformed serial killer, but he is also known as particularly powerful for pregnant women. Buddhist women are likely to call upon him when they need help in childbirth. This reliance comes from a story of Aṅgulimāla's later life, after he'd been a monk for some time. Every day he went on alms rounds, though he was not only often ignored but abused. Those who had lost their loved ones to him could never forgive him, and some who had not could simply never forget his reputation. People hardly gave him any food to sustain him and sometimes threw rocks. Aṅgulimāla continued to go on alms round, understanding it as a duty to offer people the opportunity to give generously despite the complications. One day Aṅgulimāla saw a woman having difficulty giving birth to a deformed child; he heard her call out in pain. He was struck by her pain, and compassion inspired him to ask the Buddha what he might do. The Buddha, calling on the traditional power of a spoken truth, advised him to go and say to the woman, "Sister, since I was born, I do not recall that I have ever intentionally deprived a being of life. By this truth may you be well and may your infant be well!" When Aṅgulimāla pointed out to the Buddha that his statement was simply not true, the Buddha advised him to say to her, "Sister, since I was born with the noble birth [became a monk], I do not recall that I have ever intentionally deprived a living being of life. By this truth, may you be well and may your infant be well."[1] Both the woman and the child recovered because of the strength of this spoken truth of non-harm, and not long afterwards Aṅgulimāla became enlightened.

Two aspects of this part of the story move me as a teacher. One is the motif of birth—education is a moment-to-moment birth. Each moment as we try to grow in wisdom and compassion, we become new and different people. So at each moment a person can become a wholly different person, and that rapid change and its potential should be recognized by any teacher. This birthing aspect of the story emphasizes the transience of each of our definitions of ourselves. We change moment-to-moment—that's what learning is. It's what we live for. It's the joy of students and teachers alike. The birth here is not (just like most moments of education) painless, and the child, the fruit of that birthing, is not somehow perfect. Yet Aṅgulimāla's role lessened the pain and helped bring about good results. A teacher's role is often about creating a dramatic moment of coming-into-being and then lessening the pain and drawing attention to the result.

This birthing aspect of the story also highlights the conflicting roles of the teacher as one who causes and relieves pain for the sake of learning. My students take exams, read demanding texts, and participate in intellectually, emotionally, physically, and socially uncomfortable fieldtrips. They write papers, design and implement projects, give presentations, and create and take roles in skits, which often involve pain or at least discomfort, because I, supported by an institutional and societal structure, make them do so. My students also have intellectual, emotional, and social breakthroughs, and they sometimes make great grades—these things give them pleasure. For my part, students repeatedly (directly and indirectly) teach me not only about modern culture and all the wonders of what they're learning in their other classes, but also about humility and the limits of my own view.

The birth motif that so emphasizes change contrasts with the other motif that fascinates me in the story—the theme of commitment, or resisting at least some ways of change. One of the fuels feeding Aṅgulimāla's learning is his commitment to a helpful path. It's by the strength of his commitment to his new life as a monk after murdering so many that he is able to give a statement of non-harm that has the power to heal. And it's that commitment that allowed him to hear the cries of a woman in childbirth as worthy of compassion to begin with. In his earlier circumstance, she would have been just another potential finger donor for his necklace. So while we recognize the moment-to-moment birth of each of us in teaching and learning, we also try to remain steadily committed to the process of education itself, to the process of this birth-giving we engage in together, wherein you are giving birth to your new self and I am giving birth to my new self and we are being each other's midwives as we do so.

Too often students lose sight of the commitment to learning that is the ideal of education. Caught up in the details of course and institutional requirements (and perhaps distracted by compelling aspects of student culture), they become blind to the reasons these requirements were created: to help them create a life centered on learning. Few high school and college students can articulate what their commitments as learners are.

Another aspect of this part of Aṅgulimāla's story that strikes me has to do with the Buddha's forgetfulness at one point. When at first Aṅgulimāla approaches the Buddha about the pain and danger of the woman and her child, the Buddha tells him to lean on the strength of his never having knowingly caused something to die. Aṅgulimāla rightly objects to this, saying that it would be a deliberate lie. In fact since he was born he had quite intentionally destroyed not just any being but 999 human beings' lives. The text tells us the Buddha replies to Aṅgulimāla's objection by simply changing the phrasing to make it a true statement: since Aṅgulimāla's *noble* birth, his birth as a monk, he hasn't harmed anyone.

Why would the Buddha misspeak at first?

One reason leaps to my mind: it has to do with a quality of teaching I refer to as wise forgetting. It's when you forget (intentionally or not?) that a student failed to follow through on an obligation, failed to send an e-mail when he or she promised, failed to lend a study sheet to another student, failed to attend on a day a quiz was planned. It's a sort of letting-it-slide, a commitment to the best part of a student, the part which might show itself in the future, given room enough.

I once gave much leeway to a student, Maryann. Time after time, she didn't submit her assignments. Repeatedly we had conversations in my office. By the exam period, she had already technically failed the course. She had not met the requirements outlined in the syllabus. She kept promising me a final paper, however. When I had checked in on her during the exam period, my skepticism was not allayed. Unable to endure her current housing situation and the harsh treatment of her housemates, she was camped out in the office of a faculty colleague. Not only had she technically failed the course already, but her workspace promised nothing—the office was a maelstrom of books and papers that covered all available surfaces. Maryann managed to submit her paper, however, and I read it. It was one of the best I've ever read, a phoenix from the ashes. Thank goodness I put aside my memories of her failures and the strict requirements of the course.

There are dangers to this sort of forgetting, to be sure. It can be motivated by sloth, for example. The teacher simply does not want to have that conversation with the student, the one that calls for him to be stern and truthful and patient as he notes the failure on the student's part. Or it can grow from delusion—the desire to live in a fantasy land where all students are wonderful all the time.

But it can also be motivated by trust in potential. By forgiveness and compassion. And it can allow a powerful and simple truth-telling on the student's part—the kind of simple truth-telling that indicates real learning. When the Buddha suggests that Aṅgulimāla say that he cannot recall ever harming another being since he was born, Aṅgulimāla has the opportunity to correct the Buddha, to say that in fact he has harmed beings knowingly in his life. That's a strong recognition, a strong perception, a strong truth. That Aṅgulimāla could say that truth simply and directly says a lot about Aṅgulimāla and how far he has come from his days of killing.

In a way his truth is true for every single one of us. We have, each one of us, harmed others. In this way we're all in the same boat—another implication of paṭicca-samuppāda.

Every once in a while I have found it helpful to consider what my pedagogical narrative is, as I have done here. What is the story to which I find myself returning again and again when I ponder teaching and learning? Knowing that I do, in fact, have central stories that play a role in how I conceive of what teaching is and how it relates to my life and the lives of my students and those around me helps me be more aware of some of the deeper elements of pedagogy. Recognizing these deeper elements and playing with them can lead to more honest, reflective, and deeper teaching.

It's absurd, of course, in this fast-paced world, to consider taking the time to discern your current central pedagogical narrative and to deeply reflect on it. But of course really, it's absurd to surrender to a fast-paced world that doesn't allow you to deeply reflect on one of the most important aspects of your life: your daily work. It's absurd *not* to take the time. By taking the time to reflect in this kind of way, you make sure your life has meaning: you check your anchor to make sure some errant wind doesn't send you far from where you mean to be, crashing against a rocky shore. By reflecting on the story of Aṅgulimāla, I remind myself of important truths—that students and teachers can unwittingly cause each other great harm, perhaps especially when their actions are not motivated by generosity, loving-kindness, compassion, and altruistic joy, informed by clarity and understanding. I remind myself that the greatest challenges can yield the greatest learning, that every person's context at least partially defines them, that education is moment-to-moment birthing, that commitment can yield great power, and that careful forgetfulness can allow the telling of powerful truths.

And of course I am reminded to beware allowing envy and wrong perceptions to lead to asking grisly gifts of students.[5]

CHAPTER 6

Letting Women Into the Order

Learning from Students

*Buddhism is practiced at the point where the mind meets life; it is practiced
in the mind as the mind is stimulated by life; and it is practiced in life
where the mind learns everything it knows.*
—Master Hsing Yun in *Being Good: Buddhist Ethics for Everyday Life*

One afternoon as we began our Buddhism and the Environment seminar, I relaxed into one of the chairs and asked the students how the class was going for them. "Dr. Brown, the Plant Companionship Experiment is not working for me," said one student.

I sat up, alarmed. The PCE, as we referred to it, was the assignment of choosing one plant—in this case, a tree—and spending at least an hour each week with it throughout the semester.[1] The student could sit quietly with the tree, read a book, study, exercise, write a letter to a friend, whatever. But the two of them had to be together for an hour a week. I had initiated the PCE to help the students cultivate a relationship with nature and to give them an opportunity to reflect on the relationship they already had with nature. If students in this Buddhism and the Environment class were to understand how Buddhist theorists and environmental activists contributed to the study of the environment and the responses to environmental concerns, they needed to understand their own relationship (or lack thereof) with the environment. I hadn't really thought through what sort of expectations I had, however. I didn't know what success meant in the case of this experiment.

I settled back in my chair, curious and amused but maybe with some defensiveness underneath the safer inclinations. I asked, "What would it look like if the PCE *were* working?" After all, the student clearly had expectations that were not being met.

After a bit of stumbling, the student revealed that her disappointment was in the affective aspect of her relationship with her tree: "I don't feel anything." I opened the floor to other comments about the PCE to get a better general sense of how it was going.

"Well, I have the opposite problem. I feel something," one student said, "but what I feel is *accused* by my tree. I don't feel I'm worthy. I feel as though my tree thinks I'm stupid."

"I feel very close to my tree," another student told us.

The responses to the PCE ranged considerably, and students admitted that they had read their tree a poem, that they'd written a letter to their tree, that they had introduced their tree to a friend. Besides these examples of how these people had cultivated their relationship with their trees, I didn't have much to offer that initial speaker. I simply had neither anticipated a student might not feel anything in relation to his or her tree, nor had I anticipated that lack of feeling would be perceived as a problem. (And so quickly! This was quite early on in the semester.)

Then I went home. I felt rather free as I would not teach for a day or two, and I found myself wondering what I needed to do to help my students have healthy, emotionally complex relationships with their trees. I took out my copy of *Getting the Love You Want: A Guide for Couples*[2] and chortled as I reworked some of the exercises one can use in one's committed relationship with another person to keep intimacy alive and well. As I composed the document, "Enlivening Your Relationship with Your Plant," I had little intention of handing it to my students. It was a joke, right? But it kind of wasn't a joke, because the exercises in that book do work to improve intimacy, and some of the exercises I was developing really would help my students develop a better, more rewarding relationship with their trees.[3] When I handed the students copies of the document the following Monday, I did so with a self-consciously cavalier attitude, enjoying the lark but also wondering if I'd gone over an edge. I'm still not sure about what I wanted in making the document, but the student was right to complain—no sense sitting there feeling nothing for an hour a week with a plant. And I was right to give what I could.

Learning, commitment to and practice of the discipline of learning, is the foremost obligation of a teacher. The Buddha, as

the quintessential teacher of Buddhism, is often praised and presented as complete, as the "perfectly enlightened one," but stories
from the texts defy a rigid conception of perfection. Like all good
teachers, the Buddha learned all the time and took suggestions
from others. The story of the Buddha's allowing women into his
order illustrates this well. Three times the Buddha's caregiver
and aunt, Mahāpajāpatī Gotamī, begged him to allow women to
go forth from home to homelessness under him. Three times the
Buddha dismissed her: "Enough, Gotamī, do not ask . . ." Gotamī
and some other women then demonstrated their commitment by
cutting off their hair and putting on the yellow robes. They followed the Buddha. Gotamī's feet swelled, her arms and legs
were covered in dust, and tears ran down her face. Seeing her,
the Buddha's assistant, Ānanda, was moved by compassion but
when he approached the Buddha, the Buddha refused again.
Ānanda asked a different way—emphasizing how the life of
homelessness is more conducive to enlightenment and that the
Buddha wouldn't want to get in the way of anyone's enlightenment by not allowing them to go homeless, yes? And didn't he
owe his aunt something, she who "was his nurse, his foster
mother, his giver of milk," the one who had breastfed him after
his mother's death?

On the basis of these arguments, the Buddha accepted women
into the order.[4]

The Buddha also learned from his other relatives, including
his father. After the Buddha was enlightened and was teaching,
the woman who had been his wife before he abandoned his family approached him with their son, Rāhula. She pushed him forward and said, "Go and ask for your inheritance." The boy did,
but the Buddha did not give his son material wealth or social
status. Rather, the Buddha gave him a new conception of the inheritance—the holy life. He invited the boy, too, to go from home
to homelessness, to abandon his family and seek spiritual growth
and a meaningful life under the Buddha's tutelage.

As a result, the Buddha's father suffered. First his own son
had gone forth, then another young male relative, Nanda, and
then his grandson. The Buddha's father approached the Buddha
and told him of his pain in losing so many loved ones to the
homeless life. He explained to his son that the love one feels for
others can go "to the marrow of bones" and asked his son a favor.

As a result of this, the Buddha made a new rule: that one has to have parental permission to go forth.[5]

Inspired similarly by the problems of my students, I had a wonderfully creative afternoon when I worked on those intimacy exercises for my students with their plants, and I spoke about it when I gave a talk to other faculty members describing the class. A botanist spoke up, "Sid, I see how you encourage your students to develop relationships with trees, but who really speaks for the trees? Do these people really know anything about trees?"[6]

I was caught, of course. In fact, when designing the PCE and writing the exercises, I had been face-to-face with this problem. After all, a large part of intimacy is listening to the voice of the other (no matter what form that voice takes) and loving the details of that other. Knowledge of botany would allow students to listen to the voices of their plants and help them know which details they could notice. Botany could help them love a certain kind of detail, but I knew nothing about botany, so I was unable to help them. Nor could I make sure someone else did—what botanist had the time to help these students understand their diverse plants spread all over campus? Recognizing the importance of knowing more about plants but unable to help the students do this, I had encouraged my students to seek out help from students, professors, and staff who could help them identify their trees. A few were able to recruit knowledgeable friends to help them, but most of them knew no one with the right kind of knowledge. Thus, they didn't know much about what science could offer their intimacy with their trees.

I admitted the problem with some shame, and the botany professor suggested that his advanced botany students pair up with my students and do a little report on the students' trees for the sake of both classes. My students would learn more details to help them with their intimacy; his students would have a chance to apply their knowledge.

This turned out to be a wonderful solution—not only did the botanist and I now have the foundation for a good learning relationship, but the students of the different classes now came together to learn from each other. Also, of course, we learned about trees:

- The tree of one student was actually dead—she couldn't tell that from the way the tree was situated on the edge of a bluff, blending in with some nearby trees. (After she learned this, she had the opportunity to contemplate death.)
- Another student's tree was dying—was, as the botany professor reported, "already dead but didn't know it yet."
- The bush of one student was an invasive species, one we'd all be better off without.
- The shape of one tree had been determined by a storm. When its main branches had blown off, a lesser branch had grown to be a main branch. While it looked like the trunk of the tree bent at a 90 degree angle, really the one branch remaining after the storm had taken over all the sun-collecting duties for the tree.

A tree does a lot of what it does, forms itself into the shape it does, largely because of its inability to move. What a fascinating truth. This truth relates to the comment by one of the students at the beginning of the whole exploration. The student who felt accused by her tree explained it in these terms: the tree was over a hundred years old, it had stayed in this one place for all those years, it was firm in its existence right there, where it was. The student, only eighteen years old at the time, felt flighty in comparison, she felt that she was impudent to try to establish a relationship with something so strong, so steady. She was a gnat in comparison.

* * *

I had just dismissed class and was approaching a student who clearly wanted to talk with me. Genuinely curious, she asked, "Dr. Brown, if Buddhism is all about giving up desire, then why are you wearing such nice earrings?" A shot of adrenalin coursed through my body so that I was both paralyzed and shaking simultaneously. I reached up immediately with my right hand and grasped one of my earrings to determine which ones I was wearing. In my head, I defended myself: "These were a gift from my father." (What better way to show filial gratitude than to wear them?) Well, what was I supposed to say then? I am a half-assed Buddhist? I am a lay person, not a monastic, so I don't take that whole desire thing as seriously? I have integrity most of the time but about earrings I'm weak? (Not true, as it turns out—I'm much weaker when it comes to cycling gear.)

Because of all the emotions I felt, I answered the student's question as you would swat a fly from your eyes. It was emergency defense, I don't even remember what I said. In the days that followed, I thought a lot about learning and how learning happened. I knew this student's question was a significant learning moment for me and maybe for the class. But everything would depend now on what I did with the experience. I found myself creating a chart to understand how this sort of negative emotional learning occurs as a result of negotiating negative emotional waters. I even ran out and got a huge piece of cardboard and went at it with markers. As I drew, I began to understand how positive emotional learning occurs. I found the chart helpful and clarifying and a good reminder of how important what one does with one's mind *after* a negative experience is. The diagram also indicates how more emotionally positive experiences work. (See Figure 1.)

What the chart does not express is that anger often has a truthfulness to it that can lead to learning. After all, anger can show injustice. Anger can shine a light on wrong that needs to be righted. It's not that anger, after all, is *wrong*. In fact, sometimes, maybe even often, it's quite right. The trick is to allow anger to reveal truth and then let that truth live in a way that is authentic and alive instead of paralyzing or blinding.

We always want to get out of pain, to have pleasure. And today in particular there are countless ways to do that, to escape and blind and deafen ourselves to what is going on, to the problems of the world. Taking the time to create the diagram allowed me to reflect on why my emotional response to the student's question was so extreme. Taking that time allowed me to consider what I could do to address that more personal issue. It allowed my thinking of teaching to be infused with honesty and love. As one scholar writes, "If you love the kids and you allow your teaching to be powered by that love, and if you love the world, or some small part of the world—African American poetry, physics, or calculus, kites or reptiles or music—you can achieve greatness in the classroom."[7]

What is love but a commitment to continual learning and responding?

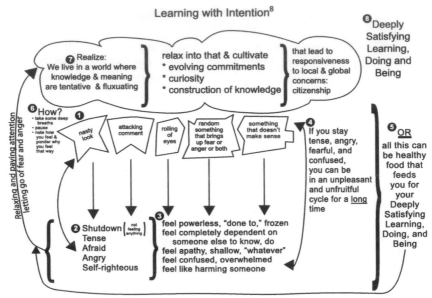

Figure 1.

Such a commitment can get pretty messy, however. One can't expect the result to be tidy. For example, that question about my earrings had helped me learn. The diagram I created clarified a lot for me. Despite my thanks to the student for asking the question, however, I think she always felt awkward about it. Her question had just been one of clarification, she felt. My response embarrassed her. Later when I read that our early ethical sensibility is demonstrated by repulsion for hypocrisy, I gleaned another element of that student's teaching. While she had thought she was merely asking for a fact, she was probably, at another level, exploring my integrity. Reflections on my feeling of threat revealed that while I did not really grasp at my earrings in a bad way, I certainly grasped at my reputation and others' perceptions of me.

The untidiness of commitment to continual learning and responding also surfaces when I occasionally use a class period for a totally unstructured activity. For example, after students in my Asian Religions class have done their fieldwork for the class (visiting a Hindu or Buddhist temple—see Appendix I: Nifty Assignments for a full description), but before they turn in their written work, I ask them to come in on a particular day with a draft of their fieldwork paper. (Many assume that I will collect these drafts, and that assumption works to the benefit of us all because they come in quite prepared—familiar with their trip to the temple, having reviewed their notes and written their papers.) I then invite them to discuss their fieldwork experience in pairs. I give brief instructions about how they might know that their paired discussions have come to an end and how to end the conversation politely and begin a new one—they may, after their first two-person discussion, talk in groups of three or four.

Throughout the next half hour, I listen to the small groups and identify stories and issues we might want to address as a large group. We spend the final twenty minutes in that large group, having a free-for-all discussion. It's certainly not the most efficient use of our time. But they learn from the experiences of those who went to the same temple but noticed different things and of those who went to different places. Questions naturally arise, so curiosity has been cultivated. They've had fun, and they now have time to use what they've learned in their conversations to rewrite their papers if they so choose. They also see that intellectual conversations can be freewheeling and fun.

This free-for-all is also quite scary. I don't know everything there is to know about Hinduism and Buddhism. Who could? I haven't even been to every site these students visit. There are questions I can't answer, and initially I found that very embarrassing. I am supposed to be the expert, and the students look to me as such, yet I come up empty-handed sometimes. Real learning, though, for everyone, requires that the humanity of the teacher is recognized. It requires risk. When realizing my own fallibility hurts and embarrasses me, I remember the work of D. W. Winnicott. In his classic article on play in therapeutic consultations, he points out that "the significant moment is that at which *the child surprises him- or herself. It is not the moment of my clever interpretation that is significant.*"⁹ I have found this to be true in the classroom and elsewhere. We are all more likely to remember what we said in a conversation than what our conversational partner said. So there's wisdom in giving students the room they need to surprise themselves with their learning. Also, of course, it's essential to help students pay closer attention to what others say, to learn to let others surprise them as much as they surprise themselves. That's learning, too.

CHAPTER 7

Removing the Arrow

Authentic Teachers and Willing Students,

Elements of Reciprocity

I will not let the surgeon pull out this arrow until I know the name and clan
of the man who wounded me . . . until I know whether the bowstring that
wounded me was fibre or reed or sinew or hemp or bark.
—Majjhima Nikāya 63.5

It was May, and our hard-earned spring had finally come. We were past daffodils and forsythia and headed into irises. I was relieved to be through with the daily public performances that were my classes. They were honest, those peopled conversations, but they were also draining. I was glad I only had grading left at the end of this, my first year of fulltime professorhood. I relaxed into solitude.

In my desire for rigorous content in Introduction to Buddhism, I had required the students to summarize every single chapter of their textbook. It was a great text, Peter Harvey's *An Introduction to Buddhism*[1] and, at our first class meeting we made our commitment: at the end of the semester they would know this book backward and forward. I told them quite specifically how they could earn their A's on this assignment—what was required in a summary of any given chapter. This weekly discipline would force them to drink in this fine book and guarantee their remembering it for years to come. What they learned in this class would be with them forever. They had complained, of course, but I had urged them on with motivational speeches.

Now as I paged through journal after journal, the muscles around my eyes twitched with pain. These journals were numbing. No wonder my students had complained. I required a summary of every chapter, so my first job in grading was making sure each chapter had a summary. To earn an A, three of the summaries had to be of particularly high quality—dense with material. I had not told them I would grade them on original thought or on vibrant questions the material had inspired in them. They were simply being graded on their ability to summarize. One after one I looked at the summaries and assigned the A's. They had wanted these A's, I had told them how to get them, and now, fighting to stay awake, I marked one A after another in my grade book.

Then I came to Pat's journal. Pat was a particularly thoughtful student. Ruminative. Eloquent. She was brave, not concerned with what others thought but with figuring things out. In Pat's journal I found absolutely superb summaries of only four of the ten chapters and nothing else. But a summary of each chapter was the criterion for a passing grade. By the rules of my own grading, this thoughtful student had earned an F on her journal. What had Pat done? What had I done? What had happened?

The differentiation between the duties of teacher and student is a haunting concern for me. The Buddha addresses it a number of times in the texts. One of the primary duties of teachers is, according to the Buddha, to keep their focus on the problem of real urgency: suffering and how to end it. Other concerns are irrelevant. If a teacher does address concerns tangential to the problem of suffering, she or he risks confusing superficial concerns with profound ones, and more people suffer as a result. The classic Buddhist metaphor about this problem concerns an arrow. A monk approached the Buddha with some questions, determined that he'd continue following the Buddha only if the Buddha answered these questions, regardless of how the Buddha answered them. The monk would stop following the Buddha if the Buddha did not answer them.[2] The questions were metaphysical: Is the world eternal? Finite? Is the soul the same as the body, or are they different? After death, does an enlightened one exist or not? Or does an enlightened one both exist and not exist or neither exist nor not exist?

The Buddha responded by asking the monk a few questions: Did I promise to answer these questions? Did you, before taking robes, decide to follow me only if I answered these questions? When the monk admitted that the answer to both was no, the Buddha replied, "That being so, misguided man, who are you and what are you abandoning?" The reply seems like a rough equivalent to, "What planet are you on?" but it's more specific. The Buddha never promised to answer and the monk never wanted these questions answered before, so who was this monk full of questions? Why did the monk think these were important questions? *"What are you abandoning?"*—in other words, hadn't the monk given up attachment to superficial concerns such as sense pleasures and petty uses of the mind? Hadn't he abandoned attachment to sense pleasures, ill will, sloth and torpor, restlessness and worry, and fear of commitment?

The Buddha then used a lovely metaphor. Suppose a man were shot with a poisoned arrow, he said, and his friends and relatives called a surgeon to remove the arrow. Would the hurt man be well served by insisting on answers to certain questions before allowing the surgeon to remove the arrow? Questions such as, of what class was the person who shot me with this arrow? What is that person's name and ethnic background? Is he tall? Short? Of middle height? How about the bow—what kind was it? What was its bowstring made of? And the feathers on the shaft—what bird were they from?

Regardless of the answers to these questions, the arrow is causing pain, maybe disease and death. The arrow needs to be removed. The questioning monk, too, is in pain, and his impractical, metaphysical questions are comparable to these questions from the arrow-pierced man. Answering the questions will not help end the suffering of either man. Rather, insisting on answers to those questions merely adds to the suffering.

How does this story relate to students and teachers here and now? For one thing, it insists that teachers recognize what's important and teach that. It also suggests that, in fact, not *all* students' questions are good ones. Some are misleading, and it's important for teachers to recognize those misleading ones and to redirect students to more important ones, ones related to ending suffering. Recognizing what aspects of one's field of study to emphasize (because they relate to ending suffering) can be a challenge, especially in some subjects. Not only that, but many fine and helpful discoveries in different fields are made when practical considerations are thrown to the wind, so this litmus test of relieving suffering can be a bit dangerous. Yet attention to the issue of suffering can give a class great integrity. For example, all introductory chemistry classes at my school are now taught in relation to the environment. Students learn not only the building blocks of chemistry but how those building blocks relate to our growing environmental challenges and the suffering these challenges cause.

Besides teaching what is important, the Buddha offered more advice on teaching by categorizing three kinds of blameworthy teachers. First, there is one who has gone forth from household life to homelessness but who has not gained the goal of the holy life (enlightenment, wisdom, the relief of suffering). Without having gained this goal, he teaches, and the students don't want to learn. It's as "if a man were to persist in making advances to a woman who rejected him, and to embrace her though she turned away."[3] Another kind of blameworthy teacher is one who has not achieved the goal of what he teaches but who teaches willing students. The Buddha compares this kind of teacher to a farmer who leaves his own weedy field to tidy someone else's. The final kind of blameworthy teacher is one who has gained the goal of renunciation but whose students don't wish to hear him. This teacher is simply binding himself with a new rope just as he's broken through the last one.[4] The ideal teacher realizes the truth, teaches it, "displays the fully-perfected and purified holy life"[5] and finds his students receptive.

A teacher, the text implies, has to have something important and authentic to give and must give it in such a way that the students willingly receive it. How does a teacher give in this way? The Buddha modeled one method when he was on alms round one morning and found Sigālaka, his hair wet, paying homage to the six directions.[6] When the Buddha asked him curiously why he was doing that, he replied that when his father was dying, he had told him to do so. The Buddha then corrected him. Yes, Sigālaka ought to do as his father asked, and, yes, he should pay homage to the six directions. But he needed to reconceptualize the six directions in order to pay homage correctly. It's not enough to bow to the north, east, south, west, and up and down. Rather, he needed to consider what these directions symbolize. The east denotes parents; the south, teachers; the west, wife and children; the north, friends and companions. The nadir symbolizes servants, workers, and helpers while the zenith symbolizes those who go forth from home to homelessness to pursue the holy life and brahmins.[7]

Honoring what the directions symbolize entails that when one pays homage to the east, to one's mother and father, one thinks, "Having been supported by them, I will support them. I will perform their duties for them. I will keep up the family tradition. I will be worthy of my heritage. After my parents' deaths I will distribute gifts on their behalf." And parents, thus ministered to, reciprocate: "they will restrain him from evil, support him in doing good, teach him some skill, find him a suitable wife, and, in due time, hand over his inheritance to him."[8] In this way the Buddha invited Sigālaka to cultivate gratitude for those with whom he had relationships and to see clearly the reciprocal nature of those relationships.

As for the teacher-student relationship, the Buddha taught that pupils should minister to their teachers in these ways: by rising to greet them, by waiting on them, by being attentive, by serving them, by mastering the skills they teach. There are five ways in which their teachers, thus ministered to by their pupils, should reciprocate: they give thorough instruction, make sure the students have grasped what they should truly have grasped, give them a thorough grounding in all skills, recommend them to their friends and colleagues, and provide them with security in all directions.[9] Not all of the Buddha's teachings fit easily into modern classrooms. Hierarchical customs in the United States, for example, do not allow students to "wait on" teachers.

Teachers, according to the Buddhist texts, must be responsible for keeping the focus on the problem of real urgency: suffering. They must also ensure that they enjoy the benefits of what they aspire to teach, verify that the student's comprehension is solid, and inspire in students the will to learn. Teachers must also work to have clear perceptions of reality and to respond to problems motivated by generosity and an interest in harmony. A story about a king illustrates the importance of clear perceptions. One time a successful king, with "a full treasury and granary," thinking all was well with his land, decided to order a particular ritual sacrifice to be performed for his own benefit and happiness. This sacrifice would require the work of slaves, servants, and others to create an appropriate space and gather the appropriate bulls, goats, sheep, chickens, pigs, or other living beings to be sacrificed. A priest would officiate. Some would work willingly, some unwillingly, and many beings would die. Further, it would be expensive, so the king decided to raise taxes higher in order to make the sacrifice. When he called in his chaplain, however, the chaplain tried to align the king's perceptions with reality: "Your Majesty's country is beset by thieves. It is ravaged; villages and towns are being destroyed; the countryside is infested with brigands. If your Majesty were to tax this region, that would be the wrong thing to do."[10] The chaplain, anticipating the king's thoughts on how to rid the country of thieves, further advises against executions, imprisonment, confiscation, threats, and banishment. Rather, he advises, "To those in the kingdom who are engaged in cultivating crops and raising cattle, let Your Majesty distribute grain and fodder; to those in trade, give capital; to those in government service assign proper living wages. Then those people, being intent on their own occupations, will not harm the kingdom. Your Majesty's revenues will be great; the land will be tranquil and not beset by thieves; and the people, with joy in their hearts, playing with their children, will dwell in open houses."[11]

The king accepted the chaplain's advice and found that the people, "being intent on their own occupations, did not harm the kingdom. The king's revenues became even greater; the land was tranquil and not beset by thieves; and the people, with joy in their hearts, playing with their children, dwelled in open houses."[12] Sacrifice is giving something up. In this case, the king gave up his plan to make a formal sacrifice of others' labor and lives for himself and made, instead, sacrifices of his treasury and granary for the public good. He abandoned one kind of sacrifice in order to engage in another. He did so on the advice of his chaplain, who saw the king's misperceptions about the state of the kingdom. A teacher, as a ruler of the classroom, can be warned against similar misperceptions and stingy and cruel responses to problems. It's easy in some circumstances to fool oneself into thinking everything is fine when it's not. It's easy to trick oneself into thinking that the sacrifice of class or institutional resources for one's own benefit and happiness are actually for the common good. (Is this particular class discussion for the benefit of the students? Or am I just grinding that same old ax I've ground so many times before?) In the face of the constantly changing reality in the teacher's private and public lives and in the face of both selfish and generous inclinations, teachers must cultivate clear perceptions of reality.

As for the student's responsibilities, we learned from the Sigālaka sutta that students must attend to, learn from, and respect the teacher. According to one Buddhist text, the student herself also has the responsibility to investigate the teacher.[13] What does she ask as she observes the teacher? She looks at bodily and verbal behavior to see that it is consistently evidencing a lack of defiled states, that is, a lack of selfishness, malice, contempt, domineering presumption, envy, arrogance, deception.[14] She discerns if the wholesome state has been attained recently or not and looks for a teacher who has attained the state over a long time.[15] Is the teacher renowned? If so, the student needs to look for the danger of arrogance and conceit. Is the teacher restrained without fear, not restrained by fear, and does he avoid indulging in sensual pleasures because he is without lust through the destruction of lust?[16] When she finds a teacher pure, the student can learn what that teacher has to teach.

According to this text, students must also check their own motivations for learning. Trouble arises when one learns for the purpose of "criticizing others and for winning in debates."[17] Such students don't actually experience the good that can result from learning what the Buddha has to teach and instead cause more suffering and harm. The Buddha compares the problem to grabbing a snake by its tail—it can bite and cause death or suffering. A student has to grab the snake by its neck to deal with it safely. In this same way knowledge can be used for good or ill. The student has some responsibility in determining that use, and the teacher has responsibility for correcting the student's understanding as necessary.

I am reminded of how often I admire students who learn for some greater purpose rather than simply to earn high grades. It's an impossible situation, of course, because first a person has to have a greater purpose, and many students just don't have that yet. Still, one can help students focus on relieving suffering—that caused by their own desire, anger, and delusion. Though the standard education system seems to reward grade-oriented students rather than those striving for ethical and attentional excellence, teachers can self-consciously and publicly undermine the system and its rewards. Part of that work is calling students' attention to their need for larger community and to the problems inherent in the system that is forming us. In the same sutta as the arrow metaphor, the Buddha introduces another famous metaphor: the raft. Suppose a person were on a journey and came to some water he needed to cross to safety and there were neither ferryboat nor bridge. He might collect grass, twigs, branches, and leaves and build a raft to use to get to the safe side of the water. After he arrived there, though, what should he do with the raft? Should he, having found it so useful, carry it around on his head for the rest of his journey? Or should he recognize that the raft was useful then, for that purpose, and so leave it there and walk on, unburdened? The Buddha recommends this latter: one needs to let go of attachment not only to what is hurtful but also to what is useful such as an insight when it becomes useless. One needs to abandon *attachment* to anything. Attachment is the problem.

To determine the usefulness of an insight, I analyze it for its usefulness in allowing me to cultivate mindful attention, generosity, altruistic joy, honesty, clear perceptions, self control, loving-kindness, compassion, clarity, and understanding. Suppose I have an insight that a friend has done something hurtful due to her upbringing. What do I do with that insight? I keep it as long as it helps me cultivate these helpful qualities, as long as I am crossing the river. Then I can let go of that insight when it no longer serves this purpose.

You can see: Buddhism has a strong spinal cord of practicality. If I use the Buddhist truths or anything I know to stir up controversy and win debates, I'm wandering around with a raft on my head with no water in sight.[18] Regrettably, I do this all too often in the academic world. When I listen to a speaker on a topic close to my area of expertise, for example, I find myself critical and nitpicking. If my emotions carry me away, I might huff and puff a "question"—which is actually not a question at all but a long speech. I am then motivated by unhelpful qualities. Examining my main point or "question" and its source more closely, I see I am attached to a certain image of myself as expert and want that publicly recognized. In other words, I want to stir up controversy and win debates.

With all that in mind, let's return to Pat, the excellent hard-working student who earned an F on her journal. Grades are not the reason my student should learn and even if they were, the grade wouldn't make a big difference anyway—an F on the journal brought her grade down only to a high B. So who cares? I did because I knew this student to be committed to learning and somehow something had gone awry. I was worried, too, that it was my fault.

When I called Pat, she didn't say the exercise had been useless and that was why she had refused to finish it. She wasn't spitefully refusing to do the work. She explained that she was a perfectionist and she just couldn't keep up such a high level of summaries throughout the semester, so she quit. She reviewed other times when she'd chosen inaction rather than imperfection.

The exercise isn't about perfection, I explained. I then challenged her to complete the work imperfectly. Use a timer, I advised, and set it for twenty minutes per chapter. With six chapters left to summarize, she would only have to work for three hours. That's it.

In this instance I learned the usefulness of sharing practical techniques like timers and received good impetus to reexamine the summary exercise. (I never required that exercise again. It was simply too long and too boring to serve a pedagogical purpose. It insulted students' own involvement in the material in favor of some false sense of objectivity.) In turn, she learned a practical technique for getting odious jobs done and, I hope, may have contemplated usefully the dangers of perfectionism and the wisdom of always beginning where you are instead of paralyzing yourself with dreams of where you want to be.

A teacher in an ideal world not only clearly perceives reality and understands how important it is to relieve suffering, but displays this perception and understanding. The students, attending to and respecting the teacher, still investigate the teacher for themselves to ensure that they are following someone worthy of emulation. Further, students check their own motivations for learning, ensuring that they, too, want to relieve suffering and not simply gratify themselves.

CHAPTER 8

Trustful Confidence
Assessing Your Teaching

Just as many garland strands
One could make from a mass of flowers,
So, much that is wholesome ought to be done
By a mortal born [into this world].
—*Dhammapada* 53

Several years ago, I was trying to find a cheap way to address my huge fear of public speaking when I tried out for a play and got a part. There were two performances and after one of them a fellow actor in the play commented on my performance that night—indicating (kindly, as though we both agreed and he were merely empathizing with me) that I had gone a bit over the top. I was not hurt by this. I was just dumbfounded that someone who had also been on the stage that night might have some way of judging what I'd done. For me, each performance was a car wreck. At the end of each one I had no clear memory of what had happened. I felt exhausted and inarticulate and not sure of how I'd been hurt and why. In shock.

Judging your teaching can be like this. While you might not end every fifty-minute class feeling exhausted and inarticulate, there is a mystery about what happened. There is some mystery because every person in the room experienced it differently from you. Sometimes a room will fill with the impatience or submission of bored people, and sometimes a room will fill with the silence and stillness of a group condemning a teacher for an ill deed. Sometimes a room will bubble with the boisterousness of students enjoying learning. But no matter what sense you get of a classroom and how students have experienced the time you spent together, there's still mystery. Every person in the room has his or her unique experiences of the event if only because of the past they bring to the classroom.

Not only is each experience unique because of the past, it will be unique because of the future. After the class itself, the thoughts and discussions of students (and teacher) will, in fact, change the memory of the event, which is what you have left of that experience afterward. Suppose a teacher does something that one student concludes is unfair. When that student speaks with another one, that other one explains why the teacher might have done something that appears unjust but is actually empathetic and kind. Then when the first student remembers the event, she might not be filled with the righteous rage that first pervaded her. She might now experience the event differently based on a conversation that occurred *after* the event.

The teacher can control only part of what happens in the classroom and very little of what happens outside of it for each and every student. Teachers can hardly control or even know the student's experience of their classes.

So while it's important to set goals and to consider carefully paths and tools that allow one to achieve these goals, letting go of one's agenda is part of teaching, too. A teacher is like an author, an artist. An author can control only so much of what a book is, but sometimes a book writes itself through the author, and always a reader reads herself through and into the book. Teaching is also like Buddhist meditation. One Buddhist teacher writes, "There is no good meditation. There is no bad meditation. There is only meditation."[1] At one level, there is no good teaching, there is no bad teaching, there is only teaching.

So one thing to keep in mind when you're assessing your pedagogy is simply that: as a teacher, your practice is teaching, of getting up day after day and standing in front of the classroom. That is the discipline that forms you as a teacher. It's the water and pressure that forms your surfaces, the fire that makes you durable and allows your colors to shine. You are a teacher, so you teach.

Some will ask, "Am I really a teacher?" Two answers: (1) We are all each other's teachers. (2) If you have a job as a teacher, you are a teacher, so you teach. Just teach. After all, despite the truth of Parker Palmer's claim that teachers are easy targets,[2] we have to get up and do it again almost every day. As Atisha advises: Abandon any hope of fruition.[3]

Cultivating this attitude of detachment about the end results of teaching is like the "faith" necessary for Buddhists. The Pali term for faith is *saddhā* and is best translated as "trustful confidence"—it's the sort of gentle, open commitment a person might make when taking up weight training. She has read some books, learned what sorts of weightlifting she should do with what sorts of weights. She has learned how many repetitions to begin with and how much protein she should consume when. She's learned how to breathe while lifting weights—when to inhale, when to exhale in different exercises. Does she then *believe* all this? Is this now something in which she *has faith*? Does she have some sort of weighty and static faith now that she's read a few books and begun? No, but she has confidence enough in what she knows to start a weight training program and see what it can teach her. That's trustful confidence. In teaching it's an attitude that you can cultivate again and again so as to try out different things and learn from them.

In Buddhism, this is the sort of attitude exemplified by someone choosing to take up meditation or to take the robes of a monk or nun. He has read some books, studied under some teachers, learned what different teachers and monasteries do. He knows in what position he should sit and how to watch the breath. He has confidence enough in what he knows to take up a regular meditation practice or the robes of a monk and see what it can teach him. He has that trustful confidence. He cannot stop every day and quiveringly assess his meditation or his monkhood. That near-paranoia would interfere in how that meditation or life as a monk is forming him. He has to make a commitment and keep his eyes open to the results.

So assessment of teaching is like assessment of meditation—on one level utterly foolish. If you are a teacher, you teach. The questions in front of you at any time aren't necessarily, "Have I done well? How so? How not?" Rather the question might be "What must I do to make sure I'm teaching the next time I must teach?"

Despite the impossibility of assessing my teaching, of course, I assess it all the time. On what basis? Frank Smith says, "We can only learn from activities that are interesting and comprehensible to us; in other words, activities that are satisfying. If this is not the case, only inefficient rote learning, or memorization, is available to us and forgetting is inevitable."[4] While I find some of this statement useful, I have qualms about other parts of it. For example, I disagree that activities must be interesting and comprehensible simultaneously. A lot of the most fun my students and I have in the classroom is implementing activities that are interesting but not immediately comprehensible. As so often happens in life, the fun part is figuring out why one did the exercise *after* you've finished.

But I do agree with what Smith says about keeping activities interesting. Somehow I must help my students engage, attend. They must find something interesting here. (See chapter 4: Do Not Cross Line: Wonder and Imaginative Engagement.) And of course I'm giving students a lifelong gift if I help them commit to finding what's interesting, to cultivating curiosity and wonder. Students must attend. If the students don't attend, they cannot be taught. (They may learn, but not the lesson the teacher intended. They may learn anger, frustration, patience, compliance, and helplessness, for example.)

One of the most important things for me is keeping in touch with the students' own responses to what is going on so I can help them pay attention and help them relate what we're doing to their lives. I use a lot of tools for eliciting student response. The quickest way I can determine how well the student is learning (without putting a four-inch nail in the tire of my teaching) is to ask the students, in a non-threatening way, for questions. I do this most often (especially at the beginning of the semester when we're all still getting to know each other) by handing out 3×5 cards and asking for a question on side one and a quick summary of the most important thing they have learned in that hour on side two. Both sides of the cards are helpful.[5] The question side often alerts me to the big roadblocks in the students' heads. Often their questions are unpredictable but easy to answer—the kinds of questions you have when someone breathlessly tells you a story without telling you where or when the incident took place and exactly who said that one pivotal thing. Questions such as: How can karma function without a god? How can monks eat if they're not allowed ever to ask explicitly for food?

As the semester progresses and we relax into our relationships with each other and the material, I can simply ask for questions and comments in a free-for-all at the beginning of class or at any time. In this way students get in the habit of being aware of their obstacles to learning—a very helpful habit because often I am teaching them one thing, but their biggest obstacles to understanding that one thing are issues I can not anticipate. These kinds of questions can be fun and startling. When I lived in a Thai nunnery for a year, I taught conversational English—it was a way for me to contribute to the community as I studied it. My students were young Thai women, mostly lay women but some nuns, wearing their robes and shaving their heads once a month. During a two-week period when I used *The Sound of Music* as a basis for learning, my students were flummoxed by an early scene when the protagonist removes her habit.[6] At first, eager to discuss what most interested me about the film and what I thought would interest them, I ignored the confused expressions on their faces. Caught in my own ideas of what was important, I didn't want to understand what was incoherent to my students. When I finally did slow down enough to listen, I heard this question: "Do Christian nuns really have hair?" Never could I have anticipated that question, but listening to it and answering it tore down the dam and allowed the discussion to flow more freely.

Another good example, one that demonstrates how long a problem of this sort can last comes from a text on teaching English I read many years ago.[7] A teacher couldn't understand why a particular student put commas where she did. She sent the student to a writing center, so the student had a tutor to help her with her commas. The tutor also noted the commas that appeared out of nowhere for no good reason throughout the student's writing. One sentence went something like this, "The elm's, leaves shone green in the morning sun." The tutor asked, "Now why did you put a comma right there? There's no need for a comma there."

"Because an elm is a tree, and you always put commas after trees," the student replied. She thought that was one of those grammatical rules: Always put a comma after trees. Where had she gotten this rule? One day in third grade or so her teacher had come up behind her as she was writing a paragraph about trees. Evidently she was making a list: elm, maple, oak, and poplar, and the teacher said something like, "Always put a comma after a tree."

That's the beauty, the danger, the intimacy of teaching—that we have all been formed by particular experiences that we remember or not, and a lot of how and what we pay attention to is formed by these experiences.

Each person's learning is unique. Learning is intimate.

In my Buddhism and the Environment class I assigned an excellent book on Buddhist philosophy—very well-organized and concise.[8] I was concerned, however, that they were learning the philosophy without seeing how it all played out in the life of a Buddhist, so I asked the other Buddhist in the class to sit with me in the front and field questions—any questions the students had. (Out of recycled materials I made us headbands with huge B's on the front to indicate physically that for the moment we were representing ourselves as Buddhists. This was fun but it was purposeful, too—to call students' attention to the difference between our usual roles in class and the roles we were taking now: Buddhists representing Buddhism.) Since the book had been on Buddhist philosophy, I had assumed the questions would be of a philosophical nature. I was quite surprised to hear questions such as, "Do you really believe in ghosts?" Upon reflection I realized Buddhist philosophy does, in fact, include ghosts, and that's a part of a Buddhist world that would attract the attention of students. Ghosts had never really been of interest to me except as part of Buddhist culture often represented in figures of art, for example, in painting, religious comic books, and sculpture. Because our focus here was philosophy and not culture, I had simply ignored the mention of ghosts in this text. The student and I answered questions such as these the best we could for about fifteen minutes, and then class ended. The other students left with more questions and more answers, and I left knowing a bit more about how they were learning.

Another way to assess teaching and determine what students might benefit from is to give mid-semester evaluations. Mine consist of four questions:

1. What do you *most appreciate* in this class? (What works for you? What do you enjoy and learn from? Readings [which ones?], all-class discussions, small group work . . .)
2. What is the *least rewarding* aspect of this class for you? (What is least helpful to you as you seek to learn more about religion?)

3. What can *you* do to improve your understanding in and appreciation of this class? What can you do to help the class be a better class for you and for everyone else?
4. What can your *teacher* do to improve your understanding in and appreciation of this class? What can she do to help the class be a better class for you and for everyone else?

The design of this mid-semester evaluation reveals that I am doing more than finding out what my students are learning. I'm also finding out what they enjoy.[9] And I'm helping them cultivate gratitude for and attention to this wonderful thing called education as well as providing myself with motivation (question one). I'm reminding them of their own responsibility for learning and helping them analyze it (question three). I'm allowing them to simply complain and inform (question two), and I'm inviting them to analyze the whole class and their learning in it—a kind of reflection I hope they do periodically all their lives.

I am often quite frightened when I pass out these half-pages of questions, but I oughtn't be. After all, what an incredible offer in good faith—how could I more clearly communicate my sincere interest in how the class is going for the students? This mid-semester evaluation is at least one way I can do that, and I almost always do it. I transcribe the answers on overheads or into a PowerPoint so that everyone's answer to each question appears together on the screen. It's important to communicate that I'm carefully taking into consideration what the students have written, so I call attention to what appear to be majority opinions and to interesting comments. To keep the focus on the thoughts of the students, I try to avoid giving a monologue and becoming defensive. I indicate to students what I intend to change in the class as a result of what I've learned from the evaluations. For example, students in my 100-level classes sometimes want questions to use as they do the reading. It's easy, with this basis, to raise important questions about how one reads. I call attention to the request and note that at the end of class I'll give them questions for the next reading. (Thus they see me immediately respond to an impediment in their learning—a sign of responsiveness and, yes, care.) Then, when we get together the next time, I ask about their experience using the questions. Often it's quite positive. They say things like: "I knew what to pay attention to" and "I could focus better on the *important* points." Then I invite the students to brainstorm on what they *lose* in such an approach to their reading. We determine, for example, that they lose practice asking questions of reading and finding important points without assistance. Then for the next class, I might ask them to do the readings without questions and during and after the reading to formulate their own guiding questions. They then get encouragement for and guidance in engaging with the material more dynamically. We could even write a number of their questions on the board and decide which five are the most helpful. What I most enjoy about using mid-semester anonymous evaluations is the opportunity for us to have a conversation at a higher yet practical level about why we're together at all: for the sake of learning.

There have been times when I have simply been too afraid to give these forms out—when a class seems particularly hostile, for example, or when we all seem to know the problems that have led us to our current difficulty and we can't do anything about them. Yet when I give mid-semester evaluations (and I do for almost every class and twice for some), I never regret it. After I've reviewed my students' comments, I always feel more motivated and more informed.

Students, viewing all their comments on the overhead, also benefit immediately. They have a less isolated view of what is going on in the class. For example, when a student thinks small group discussions are boring and unhelpful, that student might comment about this casually to another student. If the student agrees (and she might agree because she really agrees or just to be agreeable or just to end the conversation), the first student often readily concludes that every student in the room finds the small group discussions boring and unhelpful. When this student looks at the overhead and finds that half his peers find small group discussions very helpful, the student has what he needs to formulate a more accurate and complex view of the class. Often there are, in equal numbers, those who enjoy whole-class discussion and don't enjoy small groups and those who feel the opposite. Each group is surprised to find that the other exists at all. Not only do students then have a less isolated view of the class, I have an indication of what I need to work on and some motivation to work on it. Knowing what some of the problems are, I work to solve them. On these evaluations in some classes I receive pleas to lecture more. The students beg for an occasional 20-minute overview or 15-minute explanation of a difficult point. Pleas to *lecture*? If students are hungry for a lecture and they know they are and have expressed that, I can actually find some joy and satisfaction in lecturing, which I typically don't.

End-of-the-semester evaluations are another way to learn from students, but they are a bit more dangerous. There's a greater chance of scar tissue. Mid-semester evaluations reflect that the students are all still in the classroom trying to make the whole thing work; end-of-semester evaluations all too often reflect that they are under pressure and cranky. They're done with the class and wish only to be on break. So I am careful to time the reading of the evaluations. I read them alone, isolated, when I won't be in the presence of another person for a while. I remember that the initial wave of emotion upon reading the evaluations usually proves to be an overreaction and skews my perception of the overall evaluations, so I'm careful to dampen dramatic but unhelpful conclusions such as: no one learned anything at all! They hated every reading! Further, I make it a practice every once in a while to rewrite the students' comments so that for each question I have all the students' responses gathered in one place as I do on the overheads for the mid-term evaluations. This list gives me a much better and more fair view of how students actually responded and keeps me from focusing instead on one or two particularly stinging comments.

Even with the crankiness that comes at the end of the semester, much of the criticism is fair and reflective. Some of it is not. A student will say something angry like, "It was stupid that the first test was worth 20 percent of the grade while the final project was worth only 15 percent." When I have so carefully designed assignments and given so many opportunities for questions about the syllabus, this kind of comment hurts. (My reasoning for this grade distribution was quite simple: if they didn't get that first bit of the class, their grades were really going to suffer from then on because the knowledge was progressive. So I made that reflective in the percentages.) The comment hurt also because most things on my syllabus are up for debate—I give a syllabus and we can negotiate. I consider this kind of negotiation, this kind of communication, one of the most important aspects of what students do in college. Their job is to learn to notice when they have feelings that should be addressed with another person and then determine how to address them. In the case of the end-of-semester evaluation, it is too late to explain why I'd done what I'd done. It is too late to change it. I have learned, however, from comments like these, that my willingness to negotiate items on the syllabus isn't always clear. Students had assumed the syllabus is written in stone and so had simply endured what they had to.

While I was in graduate school I held a job for three years that gave me free housing—I was sort of the academic/intellectual mom in a dorm, assigned to help students understand that learning happened throughout the day, in and outside of class. As a result of this job, I often accompanied 20 to 30 students to plays and concerts and other similar events. Early on I realized I was never going to be as clothes-savvy as they were and that I would always be defining a low in that area. I decided it was a strength: I was giving them the comfort of knowing they'd never be the worst dressed. I would always be that person. It was liberating for the students, liberating for me.

So let me define a low in teaching assessment: one time, many years ago, on an evaluation of one of my courses, I was called a "douche bag." I hope no teacher has ever been called worse on a course evaluation. (Perhaps you feel the word you were called was worse. After all, it is you who were being attacked, so any word would feel worse.) Being called a douche bag is both clarifying and confusing. Clarifying in that one knows that the student was as dissatisfied with his or her experience as possible. Confusing in that none of the comments on that evaluation helped me to understand what I had done wrong. I ask students to be specific on evaluations, to make claims and offer evidence as they do in their papers and in class, but I don't always get what I ask for.

Other ways to assess one's teaching don't depend on students' evaluations. Papers, exams, quizzes, and conversations all reveal student learning or the lack of it.[10] Reading students' evaluations and assignments and reflecting on conversations with them, I try to remember to care. I try not to become numb to the criticism through coldness, defensiveness, or anger. Buddhism's focus on attention is helpful here—one needs to be able to attend to everything that comes one's way without turning away or rejecting parts of it. As attention is the foundation of a life worth living in Buddhism, caring is the foundation of teaching. And care I do, whether that's because I'm Buddhist or because I hope education will help solve problems of poverty and environmental destruction or because I really think learning is fun or because I am scared of bad evaluations or because I am obsessive compulsive or other reasons of pride or whatever, but I do, for the most part and on a daily basis, *care*. Ultimately, in the discipline of teaching, there is no good teaching, there is no bad teaching, there is only teaching. Relatively, though, on good days or moderate ones you can assess your teaching in a wide variety of ways. And on bad days? On bad days, while you're in that defeated mood, I say there's a low bar you can recognize in order to keep up the discipline of teaching: you have succeeded if you have not been called a douche bag. Having received that epithet myself, I have to recognize a different low bar: I have succeeded (in the face of the terror that is part of the everydayness of teaching) if I have once again stood in front of the classroom and refrained from throwing up and running away. That's my low bar, and I've never reached that low. With this low bar, I can always comfort myself, even on the worst of days, with having succeeded.

CHAPTER 9

Conclusion

The Heart of Teaching

As teachers, ideally we hear and respond to what is most important all the time. In the reality of our often too-busy lives, we
need periodically to examine the heart of our teaching, to make
the time and space, to create the circumstances, in order to hear
our heartbeat and allow it to pull us where it will. We need to listen to the thrumming of life inside us made possible by life outside us.

During any one semester, I teach three classes, and one or two
are always better than the third—more accomplished, more energetic, more purposeful, more exciting, more plugged in. It varies
what class it is and why. Sometimes—in fact, often—it's because
of which students ended up taking the class. I remember gathering up my books and notes for the first class of Buddhism and
the Environment, walking the length of the hall from my office to
the classroom, and hearing the boisterous talking coming from
that room growing louder and louder the closer I got. I almost
didn't want to enter; I wanted to throw the books in through the
doorway like raw meat to piranhas and say I'd see them in December to assess how well they'd done. I didn't want to interfere
with whatever was already happening. This kind of thing has
happened with other classes, where I know that no matter what I
did with this group, its members would thrive and learn and
benefit from and respect each other.

Other classes, of course, are not so wonderful. In fact they can
be horrible in countless ways. Sometimes there's an awkwardness, a fragility, a stiffness that I can't seem to break through. It
can be caused by students not appreciating what the class is

doing or it can be caused by students intimidated by one of their classmates. It can be caused by things of which I never become aware, no matter how many during-semester anonymous evaluations I hand out. (See chapter 8: Trustful Confidence: Assessing Your Teaching.) Students can be in classes with ex-lovers and feel awkward; some tell me, others don't. Students can be puzzled by methods used in the class, offended, too.

Does this awkwardness matter? Do students learn in such classes? Students do learn in such classes, but the *joy* of learning isn't fostered, and that is a problem. One of the larger goals I have is to help students feel the joy of learning well enough, often enough, deeply enough that they develop (if they haven't already) a thirst for learning. This thirst will get them far in life, allowing them to search for knowledge and respond to it in ways that make them and the world better.

So to find my heartbeat I can ask: where do I want to be with teaching in ten years? I want more of the energetic, purposeful, exciting, plugged-in classes and fewer of the awkward, stiff, fragile, dishonest classes.

What can I do to achieve that? Here's my list: keep meditating (focusing on what's happening right now, practicing letting go), exercise regularly, eat wisely, avoid overscheduling myself, continue to thrive on learning. Say no fairly often to committee work and speaking engagements so that I have the time to talk with students, to invite them to lunch, to be able to speak with them spontaneously without looking at my watch. Make sure I have unscheduled time in which to cultivate spontaneously whatever good things come my way.

I guess I mean to say that if I keep up some disciplines, many of which are countercultural (to take time out to stop every day in order to practice the discipline of really being in each moment, to care for my body without yielding to a culture of gluttony), I naturally will teach better. I will be present in each moment and speak and act from that moment.

That moment includes for me the following global issues:

- consumerism/materialism,
- poverty as it leads to death, ill health, lack of education, and other kinds of suffering,
- environmental problems,

- the complicity of most American citizens in these problems through personal choices as well as societal infrastructure, and
- contentious relationships, injuries, death, and war because of biases about diversity of race, sex, sexual orientation, religion.

So I design some elements related to these problems into each class that I teach. To do otherwise would, for me, result in inauthentic teaching. Simone de Beauvoir wrote "In order to be an artist, one must be deeply rooted in the society."[1] We are all artists, of course, artists of our lives, and we must be deeply rooted in society in order to know how its members suffer and what its members and history and environmental contexts can contribute. We must find what we have to offer as we suffer in and with our society. A teacher, a professor, must be deeply rooted in the society and reflective on it in order to teach.

But it's easy to misunderstand what it means to be "deeply rooted in the society," especially in our information-heavy age. Does it mean to be hooked up to C-Span? NPR? The *New York Times* or The *Washington Post*? *People Magazine*? The latest offerings in the consumer world? These are good questions to ask: I try to consider carefully to which journals and magazines I should subscribe to in order to help students learn. I try to consider the most effective and least distracting media connections. I know I cannot follow every single religion-related news item that comes along. I know that I cannot follow even the scholarship related to Buddhism.[2]

So I feel my way, and I ask myself, what is the most important part of what I am teaching? How ought I attend to that?

This question has given some of my classes wings with which to fly. My Asian religions class started out as a typical survey class of four Asian religions. I deepened it significantly by changing the emphasis from memorizing facts to focusing on empathy, on the cultivation of empathy by the students for people finding meaning in their lives in vastly different ways from what they're used to. Although they needed to know specific things about Asian religions, they also needed to know what role those things played in how people lived and made meaning. Then I deepened the class again by addressing some of the challenges of living in a religiously diverse society. Students read articles by professors who teach in much more religiously diverse contexts than I do. I added some interviews that brought race and ethnicity into the mix—in one, for example, Japanese Americans discussed their difficulty in saying the pledge of allegiance when they remember their being imprisoned when they were young simply for their ethnicity. It's hard to pledge allegiance a country that claims to be committed to "justice for all" when that country excluded and incarcerated you for reasons having nothing to do with your own behaviors.

Later I deepened it again by including an exercise of listening that encourages intimacy. Students were to choose someone whose religious inclinations differed significantly from theirs or about whose religious inclinations they did not know. They were to make sure both understood that this was not a time for intellectual argument or discussion, that this was about listening, understanding, feeling emotions, and learning in a different way. Whether they thought what the person was saying was wrong, right, hateful, or weird, whether they thought the person's experience was just like theirs or completely different from theirs, whether they felt enthusiastic or saddened, their whole job as listener was to listen deeply and seek to understand and empathize, without interrupting. And when the conversational partner was listening, that person's job was the same. Each person, beginning with the conversational partner, answered questions, one by one, with three minutes, at least, for each question. Even if a person had only thirty seconds worth of words, the listener was to continue giving silent, encouraging attention. The answers to these questions were to come from the emotions, not the intellect. The questions included: "When was the first time you remember learning there were other religions besides your own or other types of your own religion or secular values? What happened to make you learn and how did that make you feel?" (For a more complete description, see the Nifty Assignments appendix.)

That's the latest deepening I've done. It felt very odd to pay a lot of attention to listening when not one professor of mine in all my years of schooling (even those I learned the most from) had appeared to pay any attention to it at all. So why did I focus on listening? Well, first of all because a man from an environmental career placement company told a group of professors at my university that we professors at liberal arts colleges were doing a great job at teaching our students to read carefully, to write well, to think creatively and critically. We even taught our students how to speak in public pretty well. What our graduating students couldn't do well was listen.

Since I had been considering listening very seriously already (through relationship workshops, as well as workshops on gender, race, and sexual orientation), I took what he said seriously and incorporated a specific and careful listening exercise into the class. As I used listening exercises in my classes, I found that one of the best ways to avoid arguments and fights that too simplistically bifurcate people and overly simplify the issues is to do this sort of listening. Through the exercises, our consideration of different views became much more complicated, more true to complicated reality.

Jung once said that when you get in bed with your partner, there are at least six of you there—the two partners and each of their parents. You may laugh and thank your lucky stars that when you get into the classroom with your twenty students, say, there aren't at least sixty-three of you there. Yet many forms of teaching must address that there are, actually, sixty-three of you there. The reason John reacts so strongly to the judgmental comments of his peers in response to the video interviews of high school students on their religious beliefs is because he was once beat up after a football game for being Catholic. When Erin asks her odd questions about rock formation, she's remembering the rock store she visited with his father when she was seven. You have brought some folks into the classroom, too. That's why you take an immediate dislike to Michelle and can't do anything but adore Carlos. Learning occurs in the context of all the experiences we've had with our family, friends, fellow students, teachers, and others. Those intimate with each person in the classroom have had such huge effects on each that it as though all those people are there in the room. Learning is, then, in some ways a very intimate journey and so can benefit from the kinds of attention one gives to intimacy: recognition of risk, vulnerability, the necessity of trust, recognition of the huge size of seemingly small things.

As I continually uncover what is important, I am comforted by remembering that the Buddha himself was a reluctant teacher. After he realized (made real for himself, experienced for himself in his enlightenment) what in Buddhism are considered the fundamental truths of how the world works and how all beings fit in the workings of the world, after he realized how paticca-samuppada (interdependence) is fundamental and saw how karma works, he was not eager to rush out and teach anyone about it. Rather, the texts say that the Buddha reflected seriously on how difficult the truths he had come to understand are to grasp, how profound these truths are, how most people rely on, relish, and delight in attachment in such a way that they have even greater difficulty seeing the truths he had seen. "If I were to teach the Dhamma, others would not understand me, and *that would be wearying and troublesome to me*" (my italics).[3]

What rouses the Buddha into teaching and what keeps him teaching for the next fifty or so years are two different questions. In the texts, the Buddha was convinced to teach when a deity, Brahmā Sahampati, begged him to teach, arguing that "there will be those who will understand the Dhamma."[4] There would be a few who could understand and their lives and time would be wasted if they did not hear the dhamma. Brahmā Sahampati invited the Buddha to look at the entire world with the eye of a Buddha and so see the suffering of all those in saṁsāra. Out of compassion, he pleaded with the Buddha to stand on the "tower of the Dhamma" and teach to free those who can be freed from suffering.[5] When the Buddha did look around with the eye of a Buddha, this is what he saw:

> Just as in a pond of blue or red or white lotuses, some lotuses that are born and grow in the water thrive immersed in the water without rising out of it, and some other lotuses that are born and grow in the water rest on the water's surface, and some other lotuses that are born and grow in the water rise out of the water and stand clear, unwetted by it; so too, surveying the world with the eye of a Buddha [he] saw beings with little dust in their eyes and with much dust in their eyes, with keen faculties and with dull faculties, with good qualities and with bad qualities, easy to teach and hard to teach, and some who dwelt seeing fear in blame and in the other world.[6]

The Buddha then asked himself who might quickly understand what he had come to understand, and the first two who occurred to him were his two most significant teachers, but he learned that both these men had died. He decided the next who would be easiest to teach were men who attended to him during his period of extreme asceticism but who abandoned him when he decided that that sort of extreme asceticism was not the way. His first teaching was to these five men.

What kept him teaching for the next fifty years? There are more answers than I can list, of course, but reasons must include that he often told people the benefits of living as he did, so he got constant reminders and opportunities to reflect on why he did what he did. He took joy in the accomplishments of his students. He was able to refine his teaching, his knowledge, his art. These are the important elements of a teaching and learning life that can help any instructor flourish.

APPENDIX I

Nifty Assignments

The assignments here have been refined and varied over the years and will continue to be changed. They owe a lot to the work of other teachers, of course. Readers are welcome to use and vary them for your own classes.

1. Fieldwork for Asian Religions—Visits to Temples
2. Serving Other Fieldwork
   A. Careful Conversation Option
   B. Teaching Option
   C. Other Options
3. Wal-Mart Meditation Fieldwork
4. Experiments

1. Fieldwork for Asian Religions—Visits to Temples

In an ideal world, most students in the United States would be aware of the great religious diversity in the country. Christian and Christian-influenced students would have already met Hindus and Buddhists, for example, and would at least have visited the Hindu and Buddhist temples which often lie closer to their homes than they imagine. They would then already have been exposed to the religious diversity that makes up the world now. Most of my students (who are mostly Christian and Christian-influenced) have not visited these temples, however, and if they have, their visits have had a museum quality to them. To eliminate that formal quality most thoroughly, students should go alone to the temples. I would require students to go alone or in small groups, but the strain on the few local temples of having so many students arrive at different times is great. The group tour I arrange also has that museum quality, unfortunately, but I try to eliminate the quality in a variety of ways. This exercise is designed primarily to help students begin to see religious pluralism, to see in practice some of what they've studied, but (most significantly) to become aware of how much there is to know about religion and how varied the art, architecture, practices, metaphors, and understandings are.

What follows is the text of the latest version of the fieldwork assignment.

The fieldwork assignment:

Due dates: Fieldwork draft: 7 *March* (So your fieldwork must be completed by then.)
        Final work: 9 *March*
First you must choose which religion you want to do your fieldwork on: Hinduism or Buddhism. Then choose a site (either from the list of possible sites or from your own research) and do the following.

Part I
        This initial part of the fieldwork requires some careful reflection. Write (two pages, double-spaced, Times New Roman 12-point font) a reflection on the religion on which you will do your fieldwork. For example, What are the most interesting aspects of the religion to you so far? What do you hope to learn by going to the site? If you were to be free to ask any Hindu or Buddhist one question, what would that question be?
        Include in this reflection a few reflections on considerations of etiquette. What might you want to do to be sure to communicate to those you meet your sincere interest? What might be offensive? Why?

Experience and Notes Thereon. (The notes are part II)
        Your fieldwork will consist of going to a Hindu cultural center or temple or a Buddhist temple. While there, learn whatever you can however you can. Every situation has its unforeseen aspects, and this fieldwork is definitely that sort of a situation: an adventure. Enjoy the adventure, being sure to (a) relax, (b) pay attention to everything you can, and (c) be polite. (You are a guest, a visitor, and it is your job to do what you can to adjust to the situation.)

During the fieldwork, you will want to note very carefully the information you receive—giving holistic attention to your body, for example. *Carefully note what your eyes see, your nose smells, your ears hear, your mouth tastes, your skin feels, and your mind thinks. Do this quite systematically and carefully—constantly reflect: what am I hearing? What am I seeing?*

(If you are physically or mentally uncomfortable, please note that and try to let it go, to relax into your visit even though you might be annoyed about having ridden in a van so long when you have so much work to do, etc. Of course your emotions are very important! But doing everything you can to learn in this unique opportunity is important too.)

Write it all down after you've been in the field, beginning simply: list the date you went and with whom you went and with whom you spoke at the site. Then write your full description as in the above paragraph. Focus especially on the information you received from your senses. Also note your thoughts and investigate them. Do your thoughts mostly reflect what you sensed? Or are they more about your own history? Keep careful track of your reactions. Note your own biases and your quick (overly quick?) responses. DO NOT DELAY THIS WRITING. Write this description as soon after your fieldwork as you can. These notes are integral to the fieldwork. If you delay writing them, your project will suffer.

When you turn in and talk about your final project, this part of the project will simply be notes, and they may be as messy as they may be. But of course no matter their appearance, the experience and your notes on it are the heart of the project.

Part III: The Final Write-up
The final stage of this project is a careful write-up (typewritten, Times font, 12-point) of the experience in light of what you learned in class. The central question for you to answer is: How has this experience enhanced your learning for this class on Asian religions? (So you are basically explaining to me why and how this experience was helpful to you.) A good starting question for you to consider is, "What will I remember 20 years from now about this experience?" or "What aspect of this adventure made the biggest impression on me?" You might also want to reflect on two more questions: What might you have done differently to

make it a more helpful experience? What might you do in the future to reinforce your learning?

This final write-up is basically a personal essay, an opportunity for you to reflect carefully on *your* experience and how it has served *you*. So while you may have been taught that it is inappropriate to use the personal pronoun "I" in academic writing, you may and really *should* use this personal pronoun in your personal essay.

The write-up should be at least four pages.

What You Will Turn in to Me

You will turn in to me the three parts above—two of which must be typewritten, one of which may be as handwritten. It is understood that the notes you provide in relation to part II are mostly for your benefit, not mine. But the better notes you have for part II, the easier part III will be.

The Grading

The assignment will be graded on how well you made this project an opportunity to learn about Hinduism or Buddhism. The best project will feature careful, sensitive, profound pre-fieldwork considerations (part I). The notes on the actual trip will be dense with description and reflection (part II). They will include curiosity about details of your site as well as about your own reactions to the site. The final section will integrate what you've learned in class with the fieldwork in a careful, concise, well-organized manner, proving that the opportunity you had in this class to see Asian religions lived out was taken seriously. *Section three will count the most toward your grade, but remember: its quality is highly dependent on the first two sections.*

Group Tour

One logistically easy way to do your fieldwork is to come on Thursday 10 February to the Hindu temple in Nashville, where we will receive a tour from _____. We will leave in vans at about 4 p.m. and be back on campus by 10 or 11 p.m.

If You Can't Make the Trip to the Hindu Temple . . .

Please contact me by e-mail and request a list of possible sites for you to visit on your own.

2. Serving Others Fieldwork

Besides the temple visitation, there is one other piece of fieldwork for my class on Asian religions. This fieldwork exercise is designed to help students learn or have enforced two critical elements of conversing about religion: empathy and deep listening. If students develop these skills well, and perhaps even teach them to others, perhaps conversations about religion can go more smoothly and productively. What follows is the assignment given to students.

One of the final aspects of Asian Religions is another fieldwork project. You have a number of options of what sort of fieldwork you want to do, but regardless of which you choose, due to me are a two-page pre-fieldwork reflection, notes on what you do, and a four-page reflection. (The setup is similar to your first fieldwork experience in this way.)

Most of you will choose (rightly!) to do the Careful Conversation Option. . . .

A. Careful Conversation Option

The basic requirements of your "Serving Others Fieldwork" (due 4 May, the final day of class) are these:

(1) A two-page <u>pre-fieldwork reflection</u> on what **specifically** most interests, intrigues, delights you about the religions we've studied (specifically, for example, that might mean Buddhist karmic theory, the Hindu atman/Brahman unity—not something vague and ambiguous) or what one moment of learning about Asian religions really stands out for you. This moment could have occurred while you were reading for class, talking to friends about the class, discussing in class, whenever. To write this two-page reflection, begin by reading all your class notes, all your notes from your reading, your fieldwork, and reflecting carefully: what has really made your heart sing related to this class? Was it a moment in conversation about a particular topic? Was it a particular concept that just wouldn't leave you in peace? a picture? a story? *This reflection is written before you have the conversation, step 2 below.*

(2) A <u>careful conversation using the guidelines below, on which notes are taken</u> immediately afterward.

(3) A <u>four-page reflection on your use of this fieldwork as an opportunity for learning.</u> (Not two pages, not three pages, and not even three-and-a-half pages. Rather: four pages, full.) The kinds of questions you'll want to address are:

- What made this careful conversation exercise worthwhile? How was it worthwhile? What will make it memorable for you in the future? What do you want to keep from it forever?
- How does this careful conversation exercise relate to the readings we will do on 27 April, 29 April, and 2 May, relating to religious pluralism in the U.S.? (Thus while you should <u>write drafts as soon as you've had your careful conversation,</u> you'll want to <u>wait</u> to write the <u>final</u> version of this section until we've read and discussed these works.)
- *Be sure to incorporate aspects of the conversation you had* into this write-up. While yes, you must protect your conversational partner's anonymity, you also must weave facts and realizations from that conversation into your reflections. Concrete details are what make writing come alive.

The Careful Conversation (step 2 above)
Choose someone whose religious inclinations differ significantly from yours or about whose religious inclinations you do not know. <u>Use this</u> <u>opportunity to **get to know someone who is very different from**</u> <u>**you**</u> or to get to know someone in a different way.

The goals of the careful conversation include

- very careful listening,
- deep learning,
- emotional connectedness (to yourself, to your conversational partner), and
- interesting exploration.

Here's how the conversation should go.

You ask the person you've chosen to help you with this class project about religion—tell them you need less than an hour of their time. Make an appointment with him/her during a time and in a space where you will NOT be interrupted. The two of you need very much to focus on this exercise. Distractions are NOT welcome. (Turn off, unplug all phones . . .) (I suggest your partner and you read aloud this part of the instruction sheet so you both really know what you're doing.)

Explain the goals above, and make sure you both know that the conversation occurs in confidence—the only person who will know its details besides you two is me, and your partner's anonymity with me will be guaranteed. (You will neither tell me the name of the student nor will you reveal details that ensure my knowing who the partner is—unless of course your partner makes explicit that s/he doesn't care about anonymity.) Make sure you both understand that this is NOT a time for intellectual argument or discussion. This is about listening, emotions, learning, connecting. (You may want to read this particular paragraph aloud together.) Thus when your partner speaks, you make eye contact with that person and let go of any thoughts that come into your mind. *You do not interrupt but rather encourage, through eye contact and your commitment to understanding and empathy, your conversational partner to speak honestly.* Whether you think what the person is saying is wrong, right, hateful, or weird, whether you think the person's experience is just like yours or completely different from yours, whether you feel enthusiastic or saddened, *your whole job as listener is to listen deeply and seek to understand and empathize, without interrupting.* And when your conversational partner is listening, that person's job is the same.

Also make sure your conversation partner knows that s/he can, of course, refuse to answer any question. What questions that person answers and how s/he answers them are entirely up to that person!

Now each of you, beginning with your conversational partner, answers the following questions, one by one, with three minutes, at least, for each one. (So your conversational partner answers number 1, and then you answer number 1, etc.) Even if your partner has only 30 seconds worth of words, continue giving your partner silent, encouraging attention. Breathe from the diaphragm, make eye contact, and wait. (You will probably want to use a timer or stopwatch so each person knows they'll get their full time.) Don't interrupt each other! Just listen when it's your turn to listen. And breathe. And remember that all emotions, strong, weak, angry, loving, are to be honored! And that the answers to these questions should come first from the speaker's emotions, not your intellect. [Note: while most find this structure works, some students have found it helpful for the person they're with to answer all of the questions one by one first before the student answers them all, one by one. This is fine—just do what's right for your situation.]

The Unmoving Dominator: Occasionally a student interviews someone who, even though s/he agreed to the terms of the conversation, refuses to follow the outline. Such a person may consider it more important for you to listen to what s/he has to say than to engage in the exercise described here. If this happens and it's impossible to return to the framework provided, simply listen as deeply and as carefully as you can, aiming for as much empathy as you can generate.[1]

Confidentiality: what you and your conversational partner share together are *confidential*—as confidential as you each want it to be! You may and probably should use a pseudonym (fake name) for your partner when you do your write-up. You should each agree NOT to share what you hear with others or at the very least to be careful what you share!

1. What's your <u>fondest and oldest memory related to your own religion or to the secular values you hold most dear</u>?[2] Why are you so fond of this memory? [If you or the person you're interviewing has been less exposed to institutional religion, you may want to pause for a moment and allow you or the person to consider what is the highest value you or s/he has and work from there.]
2. What's your <u>most painful memory</u> related to your own religion or to the values you hold most dear? What makes this memory so painful?
3. What does your religion or do your values give you that you would not otherwise have?
4. When was the <u>first time you remember learning there were other religions besides your own or other types of your own religion or different values</u>? What happened to make you learn and how did that make you feel?
5. <u>Of what in your own religion or values are you most proud, or what do you most like in your own religion or secular values?</u> (This can be a value, a story, a person, an historical incident or inclination. . . . anything!)

6. What would you like <u>never said again about your own religion or values</u>?
7. What in a religion or value system <u>other than your own do you most like</u>? (For you, please include something about one of the Asian religions you've learned.)

[Note: It's painful how inadequate the term "secular values" is in this exercise. I continue to struggle with how to elicit from students who have less exposure to institutional religions the kinds of parallel experiences they have likely had.]

B. Teaching Option

If you would like to take this opportunity to teach someone about the Asian religions, I invite you to contact a youth group or Sunday school class or some such thing. Ask for whatever time you think you want/need and prepare for the event carefully. Do a similar pre-write, note-taking, and final write-up as described above, adjusting the instructions to better fit your situation. Please feel free to consult me about the best ways of going about this teaching.

C. Other Options

In the rare case, the Careful Conversation and the Teaching Option simply do not work for someone. If you are such a someone, please see me during my office hours or make an appointment so we can talk about what would best help you close out this semester of Asian Religions in a helpful way. We must agree on the option! The sooner you talk with me and the more honest and straightforward you are about the problems you have with the other options and about your desires, the better options we can come up with.

3. Wal-Mart Meditation Fieldwork

Whenever a teacher leads an experiential exercise such as this one, it is critical to give students choices. Students must be able to refrain from participation without suffering embarrassment or awkwardness. The best way to facilitate this is to give them specific options as in the "Serving Others Fieldwork" above.

The idea for this Wal-Mart meditation is adapted from one described by Elias Amidon in his essay, "Mall Mindfulness" in *Dharma Rain: Sources of Buddhist Environmentalism.*[1] He takes his students to a local mall for a mindfulness-at-the-mall meditation. Not having any mall nearby, we went (I've only done this once with a class), instead, to Wal-Mart. I did not tell them where they were going, but they had prepared for the trip by doing a walking meditation around a small lake on campus the night before. We walked exceedingly slowly in single file, working to attend to exactly what was going on right then and there the entire time—sounds, feelings, views, all were noted and allowed to pass. I rang a bell occasionally during the walk to call their attention back to meditation.

The next day we went to Wal-Mart and in the parking lot we discussed the ground rules: They were to walk slowly—as slowly as they had walked around the lake the night before. They were not to buy anything, not to eat anything. (Note: when these high school students learned what they would be doing, the first question asked was: "Is this *legal*?") If they were engaged in conversation ("Can I help you?"), they were to end the conversation as quickly as possible. We took time to role play how to end conversations politely.

I then took out a basket of maps of Wal-Mart that I had made before, enough for a map each. Each map simply gave a broad outline of the store and on each was a big X where the student who got that particular map was to begin. (This way the students were spread out around the store, less likely to engage with each other, more likely to engage in the exercise undistracted.) At the end of thirty minutes, I needed to gather the students. How? I walked slowly through the store, ringing the bell. (A stunning experience—to bring something from my personal altar symbolizing so much that has nothing to do with marketplace values and let it ring throughout that marketplace.)

When I did this exercise with the class, we had limited time and only discussed it together. When I do it again, I will ask students to write about the experience in order to reinforce it and deepen their reflections.

4. Experiments

In various classes I use course experiments to personalize the material. I always give students choices to engage in, for example, four of the six possible experiments. In Buddhism and the Environment, the experiments were designed to help them imagine how Buddhists and/or environmentalists are inclined to experience and consider things. In short, they were invited to engage in experiments that develop empathy. To get the most from these experiments, students reflected upon them at length in their journals and all those who chose to participate in a particular experiment did so simultaneously. What follows is the description of experiments from Buddhism and the Environment and from Introduction to Environmental Studies.

Buddhism and the Environment:
1. Refraining from buying
   For one week beginning after class today, refrain from buying any material object besides food and medicine. Not in stores, not from catalogs, nor from the Internet. Is someone having a birthday or other special day? What can you do or give to recognize and celebrate that without buying a material object? You want to buy that CD? Instead of buying it, reflect on how you feel NOT buying it. If you fail and end up buying things, make sure you write down exactly what you bought, how much it cost and why you bought it. Perhaps you will even want to write down what food you buy and what that food is good for. Reflect on what this experiment has to do with your study of Buddhism and the environment and the readings we've done so far. (Note: taking a candy bar from a friend and saying "I'll pay you back next week" is buying something!)
2. Meditation
   For the next three weeks, meditate for at least 20 minutes, three times a week. Keep a log in your journal that indicates the date and time that you meditated. Further, once a week write reflections on how that effects you and how that relates to Buddhism and the environment in your journal. You will be instructed in a variety of meditation techniques—some of which are standard for relaxation classes and the like. While with the other experiments some failure is presumed, failure is not acceptable in this experiment! Three times a week, twenty minutes each time.

3. Calming the fires, reflecting on nature

For one week, avoid watching television, movies, and reading anything for mere titillation or pleasure. Avoid surfing the internet, hanging around on FaceBook or MySpace. Avoid exposing yourself to advertisements. Instead, do things you think the Buddhist thinkers you're reading would have you do. Reflect on all the many different aspects of this experiment and how it relates to Buddhism and the environment in your journal. (If you fail at times and indulge in watching a TV show or something, reflect on those failures!)

4. Revering sentient beings

For one week, avoid eating sentient beings and make note whenever you use goods that are made of sentient beings. (While not all Buddhists are vegetarians by any means, there is certainly textual support for not eating sentient beings and there is great respect for those who don't.) Your experiment starts after class today and lasting one week: avoid eating dead sentient beings, go vegetarian. Reflect on this experiment (as always) in your journal. You may fail sometimes—reflect on that!. You might want to take this time to learn where soy milk is available in McClurg and trying it a few times if you don't know what it's like already!

5. The five precepts

Review the handout I give you on the five precepts. [Do not kill, do not lie, do not steal, do not engage in illicit sex, do not take intoxicants.] For this week, endeavor to keep these precepts. (Most Buddhists definitely do NOT succeed in keeping them, incidentally!) Reflect on your journal. Remember that it's as important to reflect on failing to keep the precepts as it is to reflect on keeping them—When do you most want to break a precept? Why?

6. Transportation

Avoid getting into any vehicle that uses fossil fuels for one week. No cars, no planes, no buses, no trains. What happens to your life? You might want to remember that most scientists investigating the issue claim that humans will have more and more difficulty finding and retrieving oil from now on. Scientists also note that one of the biggest ways most Americans have negative impact on the environment is through driving cars.

Introduction to Environmental Studies
These included some of the above and these below
1. There is no 'away': consumption

For one week collect and carry with you anything you might usually throw into the garbage or recycle. (Yes, this includes food waste. Please use a sealed plastic container for such items.) While you may be tempted to hide your waste, try not to. Just attach a plastic bag to your backpack and carry it around. How does it feel? Do people ask you about it? How do you feel responding? Take the time to reflect in your journal about not only how much garbage you collect in a week but how you feel having the garbage so public.

2. Water, the next oil
Choose *one* of the following options:

- The Flush Card. Carry on your person a card and record as accurately as you can how much water you use. Record, for example, how often you flush the toilet, how much time you leave the faucet on when you wash your hands and brush your teeth, how long your showers last, how many glasses of water or other liquid you drink. Try to be as complete as possible in assessing your use of water. At the end of the week determine approximately how much water you used per day. (You will need to find out how much water is used for each flush of a toilet and how much comes out of the faucet each second and how much out of the showerhead. Whom will you ask about this or how will you determine these figures?)

- Go to a body of water outside. (Lake Cheston? Lake O'Donnell? Somewhere in Fiery Gizzard?) Sit in a comfortable but alert position (spine straight, breathing easy and regular) and allow your attention to focus on the water. (You may want to keep your eyes open but focused down—away from other distractions.) Just keep your attention broadly on the water. When you find yourself considering other things (your mind becoming distracted by other homework you should be doing, friends you want to be with, food you'd like to be eating. . . .), simply note that you are having these thoughts, let them go, and return your focus to water. (When you find your mind wandering in this way, you might find it helpful to simply say to yourself, "thinking," in order to let go of that thinking.) You will find that the water evokes certain states of mind. You will find yourself with thoughts related to your own previous experiences with water.

Do this practice in silence for 10 to 15 minutes.

Afterward, write a description of your bare experience. (A simple description—no analysis. It may look like poetry or a list.)

Then write a longer reflection on what you learned from this quiet reflective time on water.

5. My Family: A Population

First, diagram your family tree as far back as you can. You don't need to include all names (though that would be good), but you must include depictions of children and relationships.

Next, discern how many children you want and add them to your tree. Assume that your siblings and each of your children chooses to have the same number of children as you. Depict on your tree seven generations out from yours.

APPENDIX II

Handouts

Over the years I've collected and developed a number of handouts that I use regularly. Some are adapted from those of others; some are based on books. Many have never had the creator's names on them, and I cannot recall their origin. I regret I cannot give credit here to all those who shared their handouts with me; I encourage you to use these handouts as you can and to develop and share ones you create.
Handouts:

1. Sleep and Sleep Deprivation
2. Draft Workshop
3. Your Class Journal
4. Estimating Your Journal Grade
5. Orientation Survey
6. Careful Reading
7. Doing/Being Well in College

1. Sleep and Sleep Deprivation

Sleep deprivation is the most common brain impairment.
—William C. Dement, *The Promise of Sleep*

We frequently assume our level of energy and our ability to concentrate and think well are due only to luck or how much exercise we've gotten lately or whether or not our social lives are going well. Some will consider nutrition to understand how we feel. Far too often we ignore what a vital role sleep or the lack of it plays in our intellectual, emotional, and physical wellness.

Sleep Deprivation

As our society excites us with more and more things to do and an ease to do things at any time day or night, Americans are getting less sleep. On average, we now get one and a half hours less sleep each night than our grandparents. While our new diversions, entertainments, and time schedules seem to allow us to have more fun, our growing sleep deprivation prevents this and actually disables us.[1]

When we deprive ourselves of sleep,

- We enjoy our life and our activities less.
- We are less able to receive information.
- We are less able to act on information.
- Our attention spans are shorter.

In short, <u>depriving yourself of sleep makes you stupid and depressed</u>. Not only do you enjoy life less and not only do your mental functions decline, but you become less motivated to do anything. In fact, how much sleep you got last night may determine more than anything else your ability to learn and be happy.[2]

Sleepiness

Hunger is a basic drive of nature. When you're hungry, you eat. If you can't eat immediately, you start doing what you have to to get food. And if you still can't get food, you become more and more obsessed about getting food. Once you get some food, you eat until you're full. In short, your body and mind ensure that you attend to your need for food. The feeling of being tired and needing to sleep works similarly. Your body and mind are aware of your accumulated waking hours. As a result, "like bricks in a backpack, accumulated sleep drive is a burden that weighs down on you. Every hour you are awake adds another brick to the backpack: The brain's sleep load increases until you go to sleep, when the load starts to lighten," writes William C. Dement.[3]

Though your body and mind are aware of the bricks in your backpack, however, the way you feel at any moment does not necessarily reflect the sleep debt or load you are carrying. When you're excited, exercising hard, or stimulated in some other way, you don't feel drowsy. You will soon enough, however. When the stimulation ends, you lose your alertness and feel sleepy. You are again less alert, less vigilant, less able to pay attention, less able to make solid decisions. Thus if you get four hours of sleep one night, you might be fine walking to class and fine chatting with friends over breakfast, but when you get in class, where the stimulation is somewhat lowered, your sleep debt takes its toll and you begin to feel sleepy.

If you are actually dozing in class, your sleep debt is huge—you are so sleepy that you will sleep in public to make sure you work off that sleep debt! Sure, you might find the professor or the material boring, but you yourself have eliminated the possibility of engaging and learning—you've made yourself stupid and depressed. Being stupid and depressed is not a good way to set yourself up to learn and enjoy learning.

Responsibility

The student's primary responsibility is to learn. Thus one of your primary duties is to do everything you can to be in the physical, mental, and spiritual condition in which to learn. Thus one of your primary duties as a student is to get enough sleep.

Recommendations

Most of us in the United States walk around everyday with a pretty sizable sleep debt. In short, you are probably among the many who are already not sleeping enough. And you are surrounded by people who are doing the same thing. Thus you are not enjoying your life to its fullest nor are the people around you helping you to do so.

Here are some recommendations to help you get enough sleep.

- Keep a regular schedule for getting up and going to bed. Keep to this schedule even on the weekends.
- Create a regular routine to help you get to sleep. Listen to gentle music or learn to do a body scan relaxation. Avoid bright lights.
- Avoid activities that excite you or make you anxious. By 9 or 10 p.m., stop accessing your voice mail and e-mail, stop receiving and sending instant messages, stop going on Facebook. Stop chatting excitedly with friends. Stop surfing the internet, watching TV and DVDs, playing computer games. Turn off the ringer on your phone. Turn off your computer. Only engage in activities that help you calm down and ready yourself for sleep.

- Make your dorm room into a sleep haven at night by making it dark and quiet. While the high population density of dormitory living offers challenges to this, there are plenty of tools available to help you—for example, ear plugs and night shades.
- Exercise every day, preferably outside. The National Sleep Foundation recommends you finish exercising at least 3 hours before bedtime and notes that exercising in the late afternoon "is the perfect way to help you fall asleep at night."[4]
- Completely cut out coffee, tea, or anything else that contains caffeine (sodas, chocolate). Or at least don't take caffeine after 3 p.m. (As time passes and you begin to get enough sleep, you'll find the strategic use of caffeine gives you double the rewards—caffeine at the right time in a person getting enough sleep can provide a very nice boost.)
- Be practical about your sleep. Look at what helped you sleep better and do these things regularly. Don't let yourself get distracted with "more important" things. (Being satisfied and thinking and feeling well, all enabled by appropriate sleep, are important.) Help yourself be alert during your working and playing hours and sleepy when it's time to sleep.
- Cut out any over-the-counter or recreational drugs you may be taking, including alcohol. Don't smoke. (Alcohol and nicotine interfere with sleeping, as do other drugs.)

If you find you have accumulated a sleep debt,

- Go to bed at least an hour earlier than normal. (Since it's hard for many people to sleep in past their normal wake-up time, going to bed early is the best way to pay off debt.)
- Take a nap during the afternoon dip in energy when you are less alert. Naps are not a sign of slovenliness. They are a heroic way to get the sleep you need so that you can be a full human and a responsible and responsive student.

Finally, if you continue to have difficulty getting the sleep you need to be alert, bright, satisfied, and energetic,

- Keep a sleep diary, recording when you went to bed, when you got up, how many times you awakened and how long you were awake during these periods. Total your hours of sleep time and notice how alert you are throughout the day. After a week of this, determine how much sleep you need at night. Most people need about eight hours. Just keeping the diary will help you maintain a discipline that encourages you do get enough sleep. Or you can take your diary to a professional and learn what else you can do to improve your sleep.

2. Draft Workshop

Title of the paper you are examining:

Author of the paper you are examining:

Your own name:

1. Read the first paragraph of the paper twice, slowly and carefully. Put a check mark here each time you have read the first paragraph:

2. As you may recall, a thesis statement is a clear statement of the argument a writer is going to make and the direction it is going to go. Write here the thesis statement that guides the paper. If there is no thesis statement in the first paragraph, read the second paragraph. Is there a thesis statement there? If so, write it here.

If not, what is the topic of the paper? (A topic is merely a general area of concern.)

3. Reread the first paragraph *again,* a third time, now that you have determined the thesis statement of the paper. Put a check mark here when you are done reading the paragraph for the third time.

Read this paragraph for the *fourth* time, this time reading it slowly and analyzing it sentence by sentence. After you read each sentence, ask yourself: Is every sentence helpful in guiding the reader into the paper? Is this sentence confusing and distracting? If there are unhelpful sentences, cross them out and write a short explanation of why they are unhelpful in the margin of the paper. (Be especially careful to get rid of any patter such as "Psychology is a very important field." or "Buddhism is a very complex religion.")

4. Still reflecting on this first paragraph, consider how else this paragraph could be developed. What needs to be said in order to introduce the reader carefully and well to the argument being presented?

5. Read the rest of the paper, putting a check mark here when you are finished.

6. What do you like most about this paper?

7. a. Number each paragraph of the paper in the margin. Where in the paper were you most confused? [Give the number(s) of the paragraph(s) below.]

b. Why were you confused? What needs to be clarified? What can you say to help the writer make the paper more clear? (Make these comments in the margins of the paper.)

8. The writer of this paper was to give specific examples throughout the entire paper in support of his/her ideas. (Concrete writing is one aspect of good writing.) Note below the paragraph number in which each of three examples occur, the source (which book, article) of the references, and what each example supports. (Example: "parag. 3, Rahula: anattā"). (This exercise is just to help the author become aware of any deficiency of concrete examples to support ideas and any confusions therein.)

9. Does the paper have an appropriate and stimulating title? (Does it introduce the topic and entice the reader?) If not, how could the title be improved? What title(s) would you suggest? Wit is welcome.

10. Look over the general criteria for papers sheet. What grade do you think the writer has earned with this paper? (Occasionally a student writes in answer to this question that the student is not

authorized to give grades or does not feel qualified to judge. Please resist the temptation to duck out like this. You know the criteria, and you have read the paper. Do the best you can to analyze the paper in relation to the criteria for grading. This exercise will help you as well as the writer of the paper as you both learn to analyze writing with certain criteria in mind.

11. Free write for at least four minutes on this paper on a separate sheet. The kinds of questions you might want to address include: What other reflections would you like to share with the author? About what related to the paper do you have strong feelings and how might you best express them to the author? Does something in the paper remind you of a story? Tell that story. This is your opportunity to relate more personally to the paper and see if you have anything else to offer the paper's author, whether you think now that it relates directly or not. Be sure to give this free writing to the author of the paper with this draft workshop sheet.

12. Often a writer actually gets to his/her real point in the very last paragraph of the paper. A writer is frequently reluctant to admit this to him/herself because to do so means to commit to rewriting the entire paper beginning with that real point. It means there's a lot of work to do. But it's worthwhile work. Please indicate here if the writer gets to the real point of his or her paper in the last paragraph of the paper.

Note: When final papers are turned in, they must include the original paper, the draft workshop sheet on the paper, and the rewrite of the paper. Writers will please accept rewriting as difficult, demanding, and ultimately very rewarding—use the comments made on this draft workshop sheet well. Accept the helpful comments; do not accept the unhelpful comments. Cosmetic (superficial) rewrites are not acceptable.

3. Your Class Journal

To a certain degree, the more personally (emotionally) involved you are in the material of a course, the more you'll learn. Instead of merely ho-hum clocking-in to do your reading and listen to lectures and class discussions, you can spark connections between your own experiences and what you're learning (and between what you're learning in this class and what you're learning in your other classes), so that reading, listening, and talking about the class material is exciting and more intellectually complex. You will want to contribute to class discussions more; you will enjoy the class more. While there are many ways to nurture this greater involvement, and I encourage you to try different ways, I particularly encourage you to do so by requiring you to keep a class journal this semester.

What is a class journal? It's not solely a diary in which you write about your personal life, though you will probably write it in the first person as you do a diary. Nor is it your notebook for the class, which for many students is "a record of other people's facts and ideas," though you may include those facts and ideas, too.[1] It is, rather, a place for you to practice and nurture personal involvement with the material of the course and play around with intellectual complexity by writing your own reflections on the material of the course. As Dorothy Lambert claims, "a journal is a place to fail. That is, a place to try, to experiment, to test one's wings. For the moment, judgment, criticism, evaluation are suspended; what matters is the attempt, not the success of the attempt."[2]

What is *required* for every entry you write:

- Note the date. (This is *required* of *every* entry.)
- Allow yourself at least ten minutes of uninterrupted time in which to write. (As the semester progresses, many will find they want to write for longer periods of time, which is good.)

Some *suggestions:*

- Buy a notebook for the journal as soon as possible and begin today if you haven't already begun.
- Note the question, topic, reading, or lecture about which you plan to write. (Don't worry: you don't have to stick to that topic.)
- Aim to write at least three or four entries a week.
- Don't worry at all about grammar, spelling, or whether you're writing or drawing or creating a diagram.
- Write in longhand or on the computer as you like. (Reflect on what sorts of technology encourage you to reflect in what

ways. Does using a pen or pencil seem to allow you greater insight? Or is the keyboard the best tool for you?)

- Don't worry about privacy—if you don't want anyone to see a particular entry, no one ever will. (Fold down pages of your journal you don't want anyone to read.)
- Make sure you have your journal with you when you do the reading for this course. Write in your journal after you've finished or as you're doing the reading. During the reading you may want to note questions or comments. After you've done the reading, you may want to summarize the important points and then reflect on those points.
- Write in your journal directly before or after class. (What do you most want to talk about in class? What was said in class that most interested you?)
- Write in your journal in the mornings or in the evenings.
- Use the questions I offer you, but also generate your own questions of the material. In fact, periodically dedicating an entire entry to generating questions is a fine way to cultivate curiosity and find your own views on an issue.
- Write when you feel any emotion related to the class—bliss, joy, frustration, anger. This practice will not only help you honor your emotions, the connection between your emotions and your intellect, and your intellect itself, it will also help you sort out why you feel a certain way in response to certain kinds of material.
- Also write when you are emotionally numb. Search for why you feel so numb; search for indications that you don't actually feel numb but are, rather, denying the feelings you have. Writing at such times will help you unfreeze your mental and emotional state, free you up to have a greater variety of emotions, play all the keys on your emotional piano. (After all, a life lived in numb resignation is a life unlived.)
- Don't leave large blank spaces in your journal—use the whole page of every page (front and back) either by writing longer entries or by including more entries per page. (Not only is this a more environmentally responsible way to use paper, it encourages you to make the sort of mess a journal should be.)
- Be consistent about getting everything related to the class into the journal. (If you write something on a napkin related to class when you're talking to a friend at lunch, tape the napkin in your journal as soon as possible.)

- Be prepared to mark entries that you think are particularly insightful.
- Reread this handout on journal-writing periodically to remind yourself of different ways you can use your journal to enhance your learning.

A word on the *grading* of your journals:

Your journal entries will *not* be graded individually. But the entire journal WILL be graded as a whole as a significant part of your final grade. First, I will look to see how long your journal is. In most cases, the longer the journal is, the better it is. (If you take thirty pictures, you get one good picture. If you write thirty pages, you get one good idea.) Next, I will examine how regularly you have written in your journal—regular entries is one key to journal success. (Journal-writing is a *practice* and requires, well, practice.) I will also be looking at the quality of insight you've exhibited in your journal, and I will look at the amount written and time devoted to grappling with class-related issues in your journal. Finally, I will look for full pages of writing and drawing and diagrams—not quarter pages lined up one after another indicating a lack of respect for the environment.

What should you do *if the journal isn't working* for you?

- Reread this handout and try other ways to make the journal useful to you.
- Use one entry to brainstorm how you can make the journal more useful to you.
- Keep up the practice of writing in the journal no matter how you feel about the practice. That's what practice is—the development of discipline.
- Read the books and articles on journal-writing noted at the end of this handout in the bibliography.

What if the journal is still unhelpful for you?

Perhaps one out of a hundred students finds the journal unhelpful even after a semester of concerted effort to make it helpful and regular practice in all the techniques and approaches to journal-writing that we will explore in the class. *sigh* Well, might as well learn that journal writing is not helpful to you sooner rather than later. But please don't think you've learned that journal writing is not helpful to you *before* you've given it a fair shot—only after a semester of regular practice in all techniques and approaches.

4. Estimating Your Journal Grade

I give students this handout only near the end of the semester. A description of the journal is on their syllabus, and they receive the handout "Your Class Journal." I mention the journal frequently in class. Occasionally students are invited to read from their journal or to share part of it with the person beside them in class. It's critical to remind students frequently throughout the semester that they are required to write in their journals often.

Near the end of the semester, they become more eager to know how to estimate their journal grade because it is often the assignment most difficult for them to discern the quality of their performance on. This handout not only allows students to assess their performance, it also allows students who have not worked regularly on the journal (despite all my encouragement) to confront the truth of their failure in private.

As you work on your journal, you might want to keep a few things in mind about the final grade on your journal:

- Almost all journals with more than 40 significant entries end up earning an A or at least a B+. Why? Because students who spend that much time on their journals end up with more excellent entries. They invite themselves to do more serious class-related inquiries.
- Longer journals tend to include entries on even the very short readings we do for this class: on poems and short stories. This is very good.
- Longer journals include references to outside-class discussions and readings. These references work in the other material, relating it to what we do in class.

- Longer journals include entries responding not just to readings but to class discussions and to outside-class discussions the writer has with friends on topics related to the class.
- Journals with between 28 and 39 significant entries generally earn a B. Whether they earn a B+, B, or B- (or even earn themselves right up to an A-) depends not only on the depth evidenced in their entries (solidly grasping the readings, asking great questions about the readings, and relating readings to each other and more) but on the evenness of coverage—are there enough entries on Freud? on Tillich? Or has the journal writer skimped on some of the readings so that one can't even be sure if the writer did these readings?
- If your journal has twenty entries or fewer, you're headed toward an F, a D, or a C. A D journal will probably have whole weeks of no entries or only one or two. A C journal has deeper inquiries but it's still uneven—some readings are not referred to at all. A C or D journal grade indicates the journal writer did not take the class seriously enough to benefit from it much.
- On occasion, a long journal will earn a seemingly unpredictably lower grade. I've seen a 61-entry journal earn a C. Why? Because many of the entries were unrelated to the topics we addressed in class. And many of the entries indicated that the writer of the journal wasn't really interested in, or willing to make any effort to get interested in, the topics of the class.

5. Orientation Survey

Your answers to the following questions will help in my efforts to make this class as relevant to you as possible. You are not obligated to answer all questions, but answers will help.

Name (use nickname if you prefer):

Previous exposure to [the subject of this course] (courses, religious training, friends with an interest, books, movies—please be specific)

What do you expect to learn in this class? And what do you hope to do with what you learn?

What else would you like me to know about you and your interest in [this field of study] and in particular [the subject of this course]?

What book have you read recently that you really liked? Why did you like it?

What kind of music do you like best? Current favorite songs?

What is the most fun you've had in the last twelve months?

6. Careful Reading*

Reading is one of the most important aspects of learning that you have an opportunity to develop at college. Reading is active engagement, and college allows you to develop the different ways you can engage in this important activity. Depending on what kind of book or article you're reading and why you're reading it, you will read differently. You will want to question all the reading we do for this class, looking for key issues, themes, events, characters, forms and images. You will want to underline important and memorable parts, make marginal comments, note page numbers. *You will want to end each section of reading by making at least a few notes on that section.* Finally, and most important, you need to make sure you're engaging with the reading as fully as you can. The kinds of questions that can help you do this include: How does this work relate to you?—to those you know intimately?—to those you don't know but could?
Suggested questions to keep in mind as you read nonfiction:

1. What is the author explaining? (What are the key themes?)
2. What are the words or phrases that have particular power, emotional or intellectual, for you? What quotations seemed particularly important to you? What one concrete image stands out from the text?

*Adapted from a handout by Owen Duncan of Simpson College.

3. What did you particularly like about the text?
4. What did you particularly dislike about the text? (Be careful with this one. Often when someone else tells us to do something—for example, when a professor tells you to read a book—we fall too easily into complaining about what we have to do. Thus it's important to answer question number three above as well as this question in order to work on a complete analysis of a text. Take the time to consider what about you might be causing you to dislike the text rather than blaming your dislike solely on the text itself.)
5. What several questions do you have about the reading? What questions do you have about the reading itself? What questions occur to you based on the reading—what related concerns come to mind? What questions/issues/problems would you want a group reading the book to explore? (Generating questions is one of the most important skills you learn at college. College education makes leaders, and leaders must ask the questions that others never think to ask.)
6. What is the author's purpose? Why did he or she write what the article or book? Is the author describing, explaining, predicting, engineering a change, prescribing a solution?
7. What is the author assuming?
8. What are the implications of the author's argument? If the author is correct, what else is true?
9. What evidence does the author present to support his or her conclusions? Intuition? Authority? Anecdotes? Deductive logic? Systematic evidence from relevant instances? (What instances does the author leave out?)

Suggested questions to keep in mind as you read fiction:

1. What is happening? (What is the plot?)
2. Who are the major characters? (It may be interesting to consider if main characters have to be human. In some works they can be features of a natural landscape—a river, for example, may play such a large and vital and revealing role that it can be considered a character.)
3. Where are the key places featured in the book? How large a role do they play?

4. What are the main themes or issues being dealt with in the book? (Is the author addressing issues of spirituality? Character? Social class? Psychological workings of the human mind? Relationships?. . . .)
5. What do we know about the main characters? How do we know these things?
6. What are the important aspects of the plot? And what are the implications of these aspects?

As we read each book, keep the books we've finished reading in mind. Be able to *compare and contrast texts*—what are the two or three themes common to all the texts? What are the two most obvious differences between the texts? What do we learn by looking closely at the similarities and differences between texts? Which did you like best and why?

You can see already that reading (as well as writing and discussing) in this class involves *critical thinking*, the great gift of a college education. By developing your mind so that you think well, you will become a more helpful and contributing citizen of the world. You will be able to make informed judgments and act on them effectively. What is critical thinking? Critical thinking is approaching something with curiosity, wonder, respect, and demanding more. It is comparing and evaluating. It's determining criteria for judgment and making those criteria clear. Most importantly, critical thinking is <u>not</u> simple opinion. It is <u>not</u> a collage of opinions. A person not engaging in critical thinking leaves a movie and simply says, "That was good." A person engaging in critical thinking will ask questions such as, "Why did I like that movie? How does that movie affect the world? Is that movie helpful to me as I develop my character? How so? How not? What are the assumptions the director made in that movie? What are the implications of the worldview presented in that movie?"

7. Doing/Being Well in College[1]

In the midst of the many activities related to attending college— those bureaucratic, social, and personal—it's all too easy to forget why you're here. While there are many reasons to go to college, of course, a central one is to create, self-consciously and with institutional support, a life that is centered on learning. You are learning so that you can be a better, more knowledgeable person. You are learning so that you can help the world be a better place. You are learning for a wide variety of reasons that will change over time. Regardless of which reasons are most relevant to you at any time, to cultivate yourself as a learner, *you must continually cultivate a life that supports that learning.* So, for example, you root your physical life in learning—you exercise enough, eat appropriate foods, and sleep enough so that you are ready to learn and so that you learn well. You also base your mental life on learning—you focus your intellectual attention on what is to be learned in and outside your classes. You establish your emotional and social lives on the importance of learning. Your friends help you learn, respect learning, and pay attention to the importance and joys of learning, your social life supports you as you get enough exercise, eat the right foods and sleep enough and keep your intellectual attention on learning. Your spiritual life, the aspect of your life that encourages you to reflect on your role in a bigger world (be it based on a church-based ritual, a creed, walks in the woods, long bike rides, temple-going, or whatever) supports you as you learn. It refreshes you and stimulates your learning.

- Care for your body.
- Train your intellect.
- Attend all your classes.
- Ask for help.
- Cultivate a positive attitude.
- Make friends in the right way for you.

Get enough sleep. Eat the foods that will help you be alert when you want to be alert and to sleep when you want to sleep. Exercise regularly.
Your body can help you learn or not. When you don't get enough sleep, you become stupid and depressed and so don't learn as well. Eating a bit of protein in the morning helps you become strong and alert; eating sugar in the morning will cause you to become overexcited and then tired. Exercising wisely will help you cultivate an excellent and engaged and creative mind, while

not exercising will dull your mind. Determine how much sleep you need, what kinds of foods are best for you to eat when, what kinds of exercise are best for you and maintain these essential aspects of good physical health.

Train your intellect.
Just as you train your body as you play sports, you need to train your intellect as you work in college. Pay attention to the practices that help you in class and engage in those practices regularly, even when you'd rather do something else. That's what practice, discipline, is. Read carefully, take notes on what you read, review these notes, write reflections on what you read. Just as an athlete protects training time by planning it into her day, protect your intellectual training by establishing regular study hours. As you do that planning, keep track of your training. Keep a record of your intellectual discipline by noting every day how much time you spend engaged in what sort of intellectual discipline. Just this sort of record-keeping will help you in your discipline. Shun activities that leave you in a stupor.

When students go from a dependent learning environment in high school (your teachers help you meet due dates in a wide variety of ways) to the independent learning environment of college (your professors give you due dates and you need to figure out how to meet them), many fail. Without structural support, students fail to manage their time wisely. Buy a monthly calendar so you can see what you have ahead of you. Mark the due dates for projects and papers and tests in bold ink in the calendar so you can always have a big view of what you need to be preparing for. Mark in the calendar other aspects of your life that you find will help you maintain your commitment as a learner. For example, if you want to make sure you exercise at least three times a week, mark down on your calendar each time you exercise and for how long. Simply writing it down will help you with your discipline.

Attend every single class session of every single course.
Your courses form the backbone of your college learning, yet you will find many students who attend them irregularly. These students (really, any student who misses even one class) often fail to notice the growing bad result. Students who begin to miss classes:

- Forget the big picture of the class. They lose a sense of where they're going and how and why certain things are happening and why these things are important to them as learners. They lose the discipline of regular attendance and the group support for being a student as well as the daily reinforcement for their identity as learners. (While they may have regular reinforcement for their identity as TV-watchers or computer-users, for example, they don't have reinforcement for the very identity that brings them to college.)
- Cultivate a careless attitude toward themselves as learners—leading to a lack of self-respect and purpose. Slowly classes recede from their attention. They're not in class, so classes seem unimportant. But those classes remain important and things are happening in them even when those students are not there.
- Fail to support fellow students as they work as learners.
- Miss opportunities to make friends.
- Miss assignments and amendments to those assignments. Professors often make casual comments about their expectations—students who miss class won't have those.

Suggestions:

- Create a week-long calendar with each of your classes marked on it. Memorize the calendar and carry it with you.
- Find the time of day you learn best and study during those times. Make sure to plan (write in your calendar) those times as spoken-for. You have regular appointments with your books just as you may have regular appointments for lunch.
- Be patient in teaching your friends about your commitment to regular study times. Because at first your friends may not understand why you are so strict about an appointment to be alone every day, they may tease you. Articulate why you have regular study times the best you can, keep them, and wait for your friends to understand.
- If you find it hard to concentrate, bring what you need to the library. Put only what you're studying on the desk. Sit erect. Try to define a goal that you can meet in 25 minutes. Study until the timer goes off. Call the time your Power Time. You'll find you use that time more efficiently.

- Many activities that take you away from your working space initially seem like good ideas (a cup of coffee, a chat, etc). Look more closely; it's often fear. You're afraid you won't understand something, won't be able to write the paper, etc. It's OK to be afraid. But don't let fear keep you from your work. Just acknowledge that fear and continue with your work. Yes, of course you can and should take breaks. But establish regular breaks and keep to them until you've trained your mind to concentrate well for long periods of time and until you know yourself well enough to determine a break that will hurt you from a break that will help you.

Ask for help when you need it.
Our culture so encourages independence and self-reliance that many people don't want to ask for help when they need it. Really, though, there is little that any of us can accomplish alone. Not only that, but professors often delight in meeting students who care about their learning so much, and fellow students may appreciate showing off their understanding as well as an opportunity to ask you for help, too. Make it a practice to ask for help early so you have relationships that can help you when the pressure increases as the semester unfolds.

Cultivate a positive attitude.
When you surrender to negative aspects of a class (it sucks, the professor sucks, it's the worst class I've ever taken, I haven't learned anything in this class), you surrender your seriousness as a student. You surrender the importance of learning. You surrender to an uncaring attitude about yourself, your time, and the people and time of the other people involved.

Every class will have its problems. Respect yourself and your work enough to solve the problems you can and cultivate an attitude that will help you solve problems well in the future. Ask yourself, What is good about this class? How will the readings, lectures, discussions, films, etc. help me in the future?

Often you will learn disciplines of the mind that will serve you well. If one course is largely memorization of facts you think you will not use in the future, remind yourself that memorization is a skill that is immensely useful in other ways and it is a skill that must be developed and practiced. If a course features exceedingly boring lectures, refresh your attention again and again so that you can get what you can from the lectures and learn to pay attention even when it's difficult. Cultivating attention is one of the most important skills you can learn.

Try to avoid making a habit of denigrating a professor or a class. You may think that this helps blow off steam, but studies show that rather than blowing off steam you're merely practicing. You're practicing being a discontented, uncaring, and unengaged person who complains a lot. By all means, explore the difficulties you're having with the class, but always with the intention of becoming more engaged in the class rather than dismissing the class from your attention.

Also important as you cultivate a positive attitude is knowing that you will fail. We all fail. Learn from your failures and engage yourself again. The people who make a difference in this world are those who, when they fall, get up and try again. And fall and get up and try again. And fall and get up and try again.

Make friends in the right way for you.
Of course you must and will make friends. But how you do so and with whom will vary considerably and that's fine. Some make friends fast, some take a lot more time. No problem. Ask people to coffee, to lunch, to walk with you. Ask them to go with you to a meeting, a movie, to explore a hiking path. See what happens.

You need someone to care about and who cares about you. And you need to seek to understand that person carefully and well and to allow that person to understand you carefully and well.

Notes

Preface

1. Robert A. Orsi, *Between Heaven and Earth: The Religious Worlds People Make and the Scholars Who Study Them* (Princeton, NJ: Princeton University Press, 2005), 204.
2. Samuel Candler Dobbs Professor of philosophy at Emory University and Jesuit priest. His work includes *Sartre, Foucault, and Historical Reason Volume 1: Toward an Existential Theory of History* (Chicago: University of Chicago Press, 1997) and *Sartre, Foucault, and Historical Reason Volume 2: A Post-Structuralist Mapping of History* (Chicago: University of Chicago Press, 2005).

Introduction: In the Event of a Crash Landing

1. I have changed the names of students in this book who might be troubled by being quoted so publicly. Further, some of these quotations cannot be perfectly accurate, being remembered years after the event.
2. That same useful functional definition: stories, rituals, institutions, ethics, and symbols that make a life meaningful. It's certainly not the only definition of religion that can uncover fascinating truths.
3. I regret that since the writing of this book the university statement of purpose has been changed and now excludes the passage I quote here.
4. Ken Bain, *What the Best College Teachers Do* (Cambridge, MA: Harvard University Press, 2004), 46. My questions are obviously based on but still a bit different from Bain's, which read: "(1) What should my students be able to do intellectually, physically, or emotionally as a result of their learning? (2) How can I best help and encourage them to develop these abilities and habits of the heart and mind to use them? (3) How can my students and I best understand the nature, quality, and progress of their learning? (4) How can I evaluate my efforts to foster that learning?"

5. I also especially treasure Mary Rose O'Reilly's *The Peaceable Classroom* (Portsmouth, NH: Boynton/Cook Publishers, 1993) and William Ayers's *Teaching Toward Freedom: Moral Commitment and Ethical Action in the Classroom* (Boston: Beacon Press, 2004). I keep Wilbert J. McKeachie's *Teaching Tips: Strategies, Research and Theory for College and University Teachers* (New York: Houghton Mifflin Company, 1999) close to hand, as I have since I first read it some years ago.

6. I have benefited in particular from these books: John J. Ratey's *The User's Guide to the Brain: Perception, Attention, and the Four Theaters of the Brain* (New York: Random House, 2001), and his and Eric Hagerman's *Spark: The Revolutionary New Science of Exercise and the Brain* (New York: Little, Brown and Company, 2008), Daniel L. Schacter's *The Seven Sins of Memory: How the Mind Forgets and Remembers* (Boston: Houghton Mifflin, 2001), Jeffrey M. Schwartz's and Sharon Begley's *The Mind and the Brain: Neuroplasticity and the Power of Mental Force* (New York: HarperCollins, 2002), and from a subscription to *Scientific American: Mind*.

7. Robert Kegan, *In Over Our Heads: The Mental Demands of Modern Life* (Boston: Harvard University Press, 1994), chapter 1.

8. This metaphor comes from Wendy Doniger O'Flaherty's *Women, Androgynes, and Other Mythical Beasts* (Chicago: University of Chicago Press, 1980), 5ff. She uses it to describe her recommended way to approach the study of myth: learn "all the patterns that other scholars have seen in other materials, all the ways in which they have tried to solve analogous problems" and then you will have what you need to interpret—whether through the work of others or by formulating your own analysis.

9. Michael Bower and Leon Warren, *The Consumer's Guide to Effective Environmental Choices: Practical Advice from the Union of Concerned Scientists* (New York: Three Rivers Press, 1999).

10. I thank Professor David Haskell of the University of the South for this suggestion made during a casual conversation.

11. An early edition of G. Tyler Miller's *Living in the Environment*, published by Brooks/Cole.

12. Joanna Macy, *Mutual Causality in Buddhism and General Systems Theory: The Dharma of Natural Systems* (Albany, NY: State University of New York Press, 1991), p. xi.

13. Professor Laura Hobgood-Oster directed me to Roger Gottleib's idea described in his book *A Spirituality of Resistance: Finding a Peaceful Heart and Protecting the Earth* (New York: Crossroad Publishing Company, 1999), 102. See Appendix I: Nifty Assignments for descriptions of each of the experiments.

14. The novel was M. T. Anderson's *Feed* (Cambridge, MA: Candlewick Press, 2002) and the introduction to Buddhist philosophy was Walpola Rahula's *What the Buddha Taught*, revised 2nd edition (New York: Grove Press, 1974).

15. Robert Kegan, *In Over Our Heads*, 30–31.

16. When I refer to the Buddhist texts, I am most often referring, as I am here, to the Theravada canon—historically the oldest texts and associated with Theravada Buddhism. Occasionally I am referring more generally to Buddhist texts in different traditions, such as texts associated with Zen Buddhism.

Chapter 1: Lie Until It's True: Attention in the Classroom

1. What Kate Wheeler calls "applying direct, energetic, nonconceptual awareness—mindfulness—to moment to moment experience" (Editor's Preface, *The State of Mind Called Beautiful* by Sayadaw U Pandita, edited by Kate Wheeler, Somerville, MA: Wisdom Publications, 2006).

2. There are many fine books on meditation available in English. For instruction on Christian contemplation, Thomas Keating's *Invitation to Love: The Way of Christian Contemplation* (New York: Continuum International Publishing Group, 1994) and his *Open Mind, Open Heart: The Contemplative Dimension of the Gospel* (Continuum International Publishing Group, 1994) are fine ways to begin and progress. For basic introductions to vipassanā, mindfulness, the meditation of Theravāda Buddhists, I recommend Joseph Goldstein's *Insight Meditation: The Practice of Freedom* (Boston: Shambhala, 1994) and his sound recording with Sharon Salzberg: Insight Meditation (Boulder, CO: Sounds True, 1996). Those interested in Zen meditation may find Shunryu Suzuki's *Zen Mind, Beginner's Mind: Informal Talks on Zen Meditation and Practice* (New York: Weatherhill, 1970) a good beginning point.

3. As a colleague writes on her syllabus on her attendance policy: "Consider the meanings of the word 'attend,' for a deeper sense of what I (and Ram Dass) mean by the pithy phrase 'Be Here Now.'" Course syllabus Studies in Buddhism 2005, Professor Grace Burford, Prescott College.

4. Susan J. Behrens (associate professor of linguistics at Marymount Manhattan)—letter to the editor, *New York Times*, 21 February 2006, D4.

5. *Vinaya Mahāvagga* 1:7–20. I use Bhikkhu Ñāṇamoli's translation here, *The Life of the Buddha: According to the Pali Canon* (Kandy, Sri Lanka: Buddhist Publication Society, 1972, 1992), 54.

6. *Udāna* 3:2. I use Bhikkhu Ñāṇamoli's translation here, *The Life of the Buddha: According to the Pali Canon* (Kandy, Sri Lanka: Buddhist Publication Society, 1972, 1992), 102.

7. *Udāna* 3:2. I use Bhikkhu Ñāṇamoli's translation here, *The Life of the Buddha: According to the Pali Canon* (Kandy, Sri Lanka: Buddhist Publication Society, 1972, 1992), 103.

8. I don't inform my students of this, at least at first. Generally, I don't tell students at first when I'm teaching a class for the first time, either. Too often they'll judge both these aspects of a class overly harshly, assuming that my not having read all the books first or my lack of experience teaching a class will have a negative effect.

9. *Dīgha Nikāya* 24.2.13.

10. Roger Betsworth spent years in the military, and then he trained in counseling and became a minister and a professor of religion. Those unique skills and interests directed by his religious and humanitarian commitments led him to become one of the most powerful teachers I have had the occasion to study with.

11. In the moment of saying this I realized how wrong I was to make this comparison—many people go to fine high schools and properly associate high schools with serious places of learning. It was too late to fix right then.

12. For more on this and other such challenges to education, see William G. Perry, Jr.'s *Forms of Ethical and Intellectual Development in the College Years: A Scheme* (San Francisco: Jossey-Bass, 1999); Mary Field Belenky, Blythe McVicker Clinchy, Nancy Rule Goldberger, and Jill Mattuck Tarule's *Women's Ways of Knowing: The Development of Self, Voice, and Mind* (New York: Basic Books, 1969, 1973); and Craig Nelson's "Tools for Tampering with Teaching's Taboos" in *New Paradigms for College Teaching* (Edina, MN: Interaction Book Co., 1997).

13. *Vinaya Mahāvagga* 1:14–20.

14. Some might have the dilemma: if Buddha is perfect and committed to avoiding harm, how could he say such a cruel thing? The short way out is to look at the practical results: Kassapa, who was mired in saṁsāra especially through his problem of pride, was able to give up enough of that attachment to become a monk, and the road to nirvana is more easily traveled by those who have gone forth. The Buddha clearly cut short a lot of Kassapa's suffering by means of a cutting truth.

15. There are countless stories of this kind of rough treatment in Zen Buddhist traditions.

16. Credit to Roger Betsworth, again.

17. Professor Susan McKinnon in the Anthropology Department of the University of Virginia.

18. For additional analysis on how meditation works in these ways and more, see chapter 6 of my *The Journey of One Buddhist Nun: Even Against the Wind* (Albany, NY: State University of New York Press, 2001).

19. From about noon until the next morning when you can see the lines of your hand without artificial light, according to the texts. This practice kept monks and nuns from burdening their communities with untimely and unpredictable almsrounds and helped the religious practice on topics other than the rumblings of their recently fed stomachs.

20. This is a paraphrase of *Majjhima Nikāya* 94.14.

21. Sister Ayya Khema, Parappaduwa Nun's Island, Sri Lanka, 1987.

Chapter 2: "Viewing Each Other with Kindly Eyes": Community in the Classroom

1. *Vinaya Mahāvagga* 10: 1–5 and *Majjhima Nikāya* 128. Where indicated, I use translations from Bhikkhu Ñāṇamoli's *The Life of the Buddha: According to the Pali Canon* (Kandy, Sri Lanka: Buddhist Publication Society, 1972, 1992).

2. Thanissaro Bhikkhu, May 2008.

3. We are all required to learn each other's names as part of our forming a community. At the end of class for the first few weeks we spend a few minutes practicing—a person is called upon to name everyone in the room. When anyone called upon can do it without error, including me, we take a rest from this practice. But sometimes later in the semester I do spot reviews, too. It's important for everyone in the class to know at least the

names of others in the class to help us become trusting enough of each other to learn together well.

4. *Majjhima Nikāya* 128.11.

5. *Majjhima Nikāya* 128.12.

6. *Vinaya Mahāvagga* 10:3, but in this case I choose Bhikkhu Ñāṇamoli's translation, *The Life of the Buddha: According to the Pali Canon*, 116.

7. *Vinaya Mahāvagga* 10:4, but in this case I choose Bhikkhu Ñāṇamoli's translation, *The Life of the Buddha: According to the Pali Canon*, 118.

8. For more on loving-kindness meditation, see Sharon Salzberg's *Loving-kindness: The Revolutionary Art of Happiness* (Boston: Shambhala, 1997) and John Makransky's *Awakening Through love: Unveiling Your Deepest Goodness* (Boston: Wisdom, 2007). For more traditional explanations, *The Path of Purification: Visuddhimagga* by Bhadantācariya Buddhaghosa, trans. Bhikkhu Ñāṇamoli (Seattle: Buddhist Publication Society Pariyatti Editions, 1991), III 57f., 105f., 122; VII 18, 28; IX 1f., 92f., 98, 119f.; XII 34, 37; XIII 34; XIV 154.

9. Loving-kindness meditation is also a lovely way to enrich graduation ceremonies, which can get quite tedious after a few years. That tedium ends if one focuses on each student when his/her name is called and says to oneself, "May Mary be peaceful and happy. May Baruch be peaceful and happy. . . ." For more on loving-kindness meditation, see chapter 3: Stopping an Elephant in Its Tracks: Irritation, Anger, and Rage.

10. *Vinaya Mahāvagga* 10:5

11. *Vinaya Mahāvagga* 10:5, but in this case I choose Bhikkhu Ñāṇamoli's translation, *The Life of the Buddha: According to the Pali Canon*, 118.

12. *Dīgha Nikāya* 16 1.11.

13. *Majjhima Nikāya* 104.

14. McKeachie, in his *Teaching Tips* recommends using the fishbowl technique, too, in this situation, but I've not had the nerve yet to try.

15. *Majjhima Nikāya* 104, fn 992, p. 1309

16. *Majjhima Nikāya* 104, fn 991, p. 1309

17. Peter Harvey, *Introduction*, 197.

Chapter 3: Stopping a Raging Elephant Dead in Its Tracks: Irritation, Anger, and Rage

1. Oddly, the underlying problem here crystallized when I read about the same dynamic one can have with one's cat in Pam Johnson-Bennet, *Cat vs. Cat: Keeping Peace When You Have More Than One Cat* (New York: Penguin Books, 2004), 149.

2. *Majjhima Nikāya* 8:14.1–27.

3. *Vinaya Chullavagga* 7:3. *The Book of Discipline: Vinaya-pitaka*, volume V (*Cullavagga*), trans. I. B. Horner (Oxford, UK: Pali Text Society, 1997), 274. The elephant's act of taking the dust at the Buddha's feet and placing it on its own head is one that reflects how the social hierarchy parallels the body

hierarchy. This parallel holds in many Buddhist cultures to this day. It is, for example, still customary for lay people to prostrate to Buddha statues and to monks (alas, in fewer circumstances, to nuns) so that the head of the lay person is on or below the level of the feet of the Buddha statue or of the person who has gone forth.

4. Many American convert Buddhists think shame is not part of Buddhism, but it is. The Buddha calls shame one of the seven good qualities of a noble disciple: "He has shame; he is ashamed of misconduct in body, speech, and mind, ashamed of engaging in evil unwholesome deeds" (*Majjima Nikāya* 53.12). The Buddha also calls shame (in the Pali: *hiri*) and fear of wrongdoing (*otappa*) complementary "guardians of the world" (*Anguttara-Nikāya*. i.51). The Buddhist commentator Buddhaghosa clarifies their functions and relationship: shame is "disgust at evil," caused by self-respect while fear of wrongdoing is the "dread of evil," caused by respect of others. Both invite one to avoid evil and so are useful qualities. *Visuddhimagga* XIV, 142.

5. I've been told by a psychology professor that studies show that in such circumstances people routinely lie, even when anonymity is guaranteed so there are no negative repercussions for telling the truth. Perhaps, then, the example simply functions as an ornately designed reminder to keep up with the reading.

6. For a lovely poem that captures this experience, see "Did I miss anything?" in Tom Wayman's *Did I Miss Anything? Selected Poems 1973–1993* (Madeira Park, BC, Canada: Harbour, 1993).

7. William C. Dement, *The Promise of Sleep* (New York: Dell, 1999), 275.

8. Gilbert Highet, *The Art of Teaching*. (New York: Alfred A. Knopf, 1950), 27–28.

Chapter 4: Do Not Cross Line: Wonder and Imaginative Engagement

1. *Samyutta Nikaya* 56:11.
2. *Samyutta Nikaya* 56:11.
3. Spiritual, too, but definitions of this word vary so much. Were I to use it here, I would want to define it as a feeling of connectedness with other aspects of the world. As so defined, it classifies as a feeling, however, and so is covered by the category of "emotional."
4. Lillian Weber of the Workshop Center for Open Education at the City College of New York. Quoted in Ayers, *Teaching Toward Freedom*, 41.
5. Mark Edmundsen discusses a similar experience in his book *Why Read?* (New York: Bloomsbury, 2004).
6. See Chapter 1: Lie Until It's True: Attention in the Classroom.
7. Described particularly clearly in Joanna Macy and Molly Young Brown's *Coming Back To Life: Practices to Reconnect Our Lives, Our World* (Gabriola Island, Canada: New Society Publishers, 1998), 61.
8. Professor Grace Burford of Prescott College.
9. Macy and Brown, 1998, 61.

10. For more on this kind of meditation, see especially Miranda Shaw's *Passionate Enlightenment: Women in Tantric Buddhism* (Princeton, NJ: Princeton University Press, 1994), 26–27.
11. See Susan M. Drake, "Guided Imagery and Education: Theory, Practice and Experience," *Journal of Mental Imagery* Volume 18 (1996), 94–132.
12. After all, these kinds of feats of the imagination lead to works such as Michael Cunningham's *The Hours*, a stunning play on Virginia Woolf's *Mrs. Dalloway*, and Zadie Smith's spin on *Howard's End* entitled *On Beauty*.
13. Williams, Linda Verlee. *Teaching for the Two-Sided Mind: A Guide to Right Brain/Left Brain Education* (New York: Simon & Schuster, 1983), 136–37.
14. Susan M. Drake's, "Guided Imagery and Education: Theory, Practice and Experience," 94.
15. Consider how different it is to label the same experience as a "hallucination" or a "vision"—the first indicates the experience is an aberration of the mind, something not normal and not to be encouraged. The latter gives the experience a context, religious, and some weight—visions are important to religious experience.
16. E-mail 26 August 2005, Professor Tam Carlson of Sewanee: The University of the South.

Chapter 5: Homicidal Tendencies: The Story of a Teacher and a Student

1. This story is told in *Majjhima Nikāya* 86, the *Majjhima Nikāya* commentary, and in the Theragatha commentary. All direct quotations here are from *The Middle Length Discourses of the Buddha: A New Translation of the Majjhima Nikāya*, trans. Bhikkhu Ñāṇamoli and Bhikkhu Bodhi (Boston: Wisdom Publications, 1995), 710–17. That version, however, does not include the early part of this story—Aṅgulimāla's birth and education. For those parts of the story, I depend on Hellmuth Hecker's "Angulimala: A Murderer's Road to Sainthood" in Nyanaponika Thera and Hellmuth Hecker's *Great Disciples of the Buddha: Their Lives, Their Works, Their Legacy*, edited by Bhikkhu Bodhi (Boston: Wisdom Publications, 1997), 319–33. Hecker's version depends on *Majjhima Nikāya* 86 as well as commentaries on the *Majjhima Nikāya* and on the Theragatha.
2. Those less mythologically inclined may be diverted by the improbability or violence of the story. Yet Buddhism is hardly the only tradition with violent tales. After all, Abraham was ready to kill his son; Jesus was tortured and killed on a cross.
3. *Majjhima Nikāya* 86.5.
4. *Majjhima Nikāya* 86.15.
5. The Aṅgulimāla story, incidentally, has inspired Buddhist meditation programs in prisons all over the world. For an overview, read Virginia Cohn Parkum and J. Anthony Stultz's "The Angulimala Lineage: Buddhist Prison Ministries," *Engaged Buddhism in the West*, ed. Christopher S. Queen (Boston: Wisdom Publications, 2000), 347–71. Videos on this phenomenon

include *Doing Time, Doing Vipassana* (a look at meditation used in an Indian prison), *Changing from the Inside* (meditation used in a prison in Seattle, Washington), and most recently, *The Dhamma Brothers* (meditation in a prison in Alabama).

Chapter 6: Letting Women into the Order: Learning from Students

1. Roger Gottlieb, *A Spirituality of Resistance: Finding a Peaceful Heart and Protecting the Earth* (New York: Crossroad Publishing Company, 1999), 102.
2. Harville Hendrix's *Getting the Love You Want: A Guide for Couples* (New York: HarperCollins, 1988), a regrettable title for a useful book.
3. In fact some of these exercises were taken almost verbatim from the book!
4. This story is a fascinating one in countless ways and includes some very disturbing elements (e.g., the Buddha declared that Buddhism would last a shorter time because women had been accepted into the order), *Vinaya Cullavagga* 10:1 and *Anguttara Nikāya* 8:51.
5. *Vinaya Mahāvagga* 1:54.
6. Jon Evans, Biology Department and Environmental Studies Program at Sewanee: The University of the South.
7. Ayers, William. *Teaching Toward Freedom: Moral Commitment and Ethical Action in the Classroom.* (Boston: Beacon Press, 2004), 51–52.
8. Informed by William G. Perry's *Ethical and Intellectual Development in the College Years: A Scheme* (San Francisco: Jossey-Bass, 1999) and Belenky, Mary Field, Blythe McVicker Clinchy, Nancy Rule Goldberger, Jill Mattuck Tarule's *Women's Ways of Knowing: The Development of Self, Voice, and Mind* (New York: Basic Books, 1969, 1973).
9. D. W. Winnicott, "Playing: Its Theoretical Status in the Clinical Situation." *International Journal of Psycho-Analysis* 49 (1968), 597.

Chapter 7: Removing the Arrow: Authentic Teachers and Willing Students, Elements of Reciprocity

1. Cambridge: Cambridge University Press, 1990.
2. This story occurs in *Majjhima Nikāya* 63.
3. *Digha Nikāya* 12.16.
4. *Digha Nikāya* 12.18.
5. *Digha Nikāya* 12.55.
6. *Digha Nikāya* 31.
7. A Brahmin is a member of the hereditary priesthood.
8. *Digha Nikāya* 31.29.
9. *Digha Nikāya* 31.29.
10. *Digha Nikāya* 5.11.
11. *Digha Nikāya* 5.11.
12. *Digha Nikāya* 5.11.
13. *Majjhima Nikāya* 47.

14. *Majjhima Nikāya* 47.4.
15. *Majjhima Nikāya* 47.7.
16. *Majjhima Nikāya* 47.9.
17. *Majjhima Nikāya* 22.10.
18. *Majjhima Nikāya* 16.

Chapter 8: Trustful Confidence: Assessing Your Teaching

1. Shunryu Suzuki's *Zen Mind, Beginner's Mind: Informal Talks on Zen Medita-tion and Practice* (New York: Weatherhill, 1970).
2. Parker Palmer, *The Courage To Teach: Exploring the Inner Landscape of a Teacher's Life* (San Francisco: Jossey-Bass Publishers, 1998), 3.
3. Pema Chodron, *Start Where You Are: A Guide to Compassionate Living* (Boston: Shambhala Press, 1994), 96.
4. William Ayers quotes Smith in *Teaching Toward Freedom: Moral Commitment and Ethical Action in the Classroom.* (Boston: Beacon Press, 2004), 18.
5. Peter Filene in his *The Joy of Teaching: A Practical Guide for New Teachers* (Chapel Hill, NC: The University of North Carolina Press, 2005) suggests a one-minute feedback memo addressing three topics: what the main point of that class was, what interested the student most, and what the student didn't understand, 15.
6. The irony was already clear, but I happened to have all the lyrics to the songs on my hard disk. The movie is about a Catholic novice nun who gives up the religious life for the family life, who gives up poverty and embraces wealth.
7. I regret I have not succeeded in finding the source for this story so not only can I not note it here but I must with all humility await learning in which ways I have misremembered the story!
8. Walpola Rahula, *What the Buddha Taught* (New York: Grove Press, 1959).
9. It's important, of course, to find out what they enjoy but not to surrender to merely entertaining them, a phenomenon Mark Edmundson explores in his book *Why Read?* (New York: Bloomsbury, 2004).
10. For other kinds of assessment, a good place to start is Wilber J. McKeachie's *Teaching Tips: Strategies, Research and Theory for College and University Teachers* (New York: Houghton Mifflin Company, 1999).

Chapter 9: Conclusion: The Heart of Teaching

1. In *The Second Sex*, quoted in Natalie Goldberg's *Wild Mind: Living the Writer's Life* (New York: Bantam, 1990), 187
2. In an essay in the *New York Times Book Review*, Joe Queenan "calculated how many books I could read if I lived to my actuarially expected age. The answer was 2,138." Given that, how does one choose what to read? "Wish List: No More Books!" *New York Times Book Review* 25 December 2005, 23.
3. *Majjhima Nikāya* 26.19. Gilbert Highet puts it more long-windedly but quite entertainingly as follows: "It is one of the two worst drawbacks in

the job. It is bitter to be poor [the first drawback he lists], trying to awaken understanding and appreciation of genuinely important things in what seems to be a collection of spoiled, ill-mannered boobies, smirking or scowling, yawning or chattering, whose ideals are gangsters, footballers, and Hollywood divorcees. It is like giving a blood transfusion, and then seeing your precious blood spilt on the ground and trodden into the mud" Gilbert Highet, *The Art of Teaching* (New York: Alfred A. Knopf, 1950), 12.

4.   *Majjhima Nikāya* 26.20.
5.   *Majjhima Nikāya* 26.20.
6.   *Majjhima Nikāya* 26.21.

Appendix I: Nifty Assignments

Serving Others Fieldwork
1.   Thanks to Professor Judith Simmer-Brown of Naropa University for helping me understand the best way to work with this problem. Professor Simmer-Brown has done much work on Buddhist-Christian dialogue as well as Tibetan Buddhism, women and Buddhism, and contemplative pedagogy.
2.   I thank Bahia Yackzan for her help in devising these questions. She was also one of my first and primary teachers of communication techniques that help with intimacy and justice.

Wal-Mart Meditation Fieldwork
1.   Edited by Stephanie Kaza and Kenneth Kraft (Boston: Shambhala, 2000), 332–34.

Appendix II: Handouts

Sleep and Sleep Deprivation
1.   William Dement refers to our "hedomasochism"—our desire to have fun is so great that we actually end up in pain because of it.
2.   Dement, *The Promise of Sleep* (New York: Dell, 1999), 55.
3.   Dement, *The Promise of Sleep* (New York: Dell, 1999), 56.
4.   www.sleepfoundation.org.

Your Class Journal
1.   Toby Fulwiler, "Journals across Disciplines" in *English Journal,* 69:9 (December 1980), 17.
2.   Ken Macrorie, "What is a Journal" in, *Writing to be Read,* 2nd ed. (Rochelle Park, NJ: Hayden, 1976), 151. Other helpful sources include: Peter Elbow's *Writing Without Teachers* (New York: Oxford University Press, 1973); Toby Fulwiler's "Journals Across the Disciplines" in *English Journal* 69:10

(December 1980), 14–19; and Henry Steffens's "Journals in the Teaching of History," in *The Journal Book,* chapter 22, 219–226. For a more therapeutic view on journals, see Ira Progoff's work, *At a Journal Workshop: Writing to Access the Power of the Unconscious and Evoke Creative Ability* (Tarcher, 1992).

Doing/Being Well in College

1. This handout was inspired by Steve Gladis's *Surviving the First Year of College: Myth vs. Reality* (HRD, 1999), and our suggestions here overlap—with very good reason! (We both suggest training one's intellect and attending all classes, for example.) Gladis' book is a very practical guide to cultivating habits that result in learning in college and good grades.

Glossary

Anatta	not self, lack of essence
Deva	celestial being, deity
Dhamma	while this word has a huge number of meanings, in this book it generally refers to the Buddhist truths, doctrines, or teachings.
Hiri	shame
Otappa	fear of wrongdoing
Paticca-samuppada	interdependence
Sutta	discourse. The term refers in this book to a collection of the oldest Buddhist texts that make up one third of the canon for Theravada Buddhists.

Bibliography

Amidon, Elias in "Mall Mindfulness." *Dharma Rain: Sources of Buddhist Environmentalism*. Edited by Stephanie Kaza and Kenneth Kraft. Boston: Shambhala Press, 2000: 332–34.

Ayers, William. *Teaching Toward Freedom: Moral Commitment and Ethical Action in the Classroom*. Boston: Beacon Press, 2004.

Bain, Ken. *What the Best College Teachers Do*. Cambridge: Harvard University Press, 2004.

Belenky, Mary Field, Blythe McVicker Clinchy, Nancy Rule Goldberger, Jill Mattuck Tarule. *Women's Ways of Knowing: The Development of Self, Voice, and Mind*. New York: Basic Books, 1969, 1973.

The Book of Discipline (Vinaya-Pitaka). Trans. I. B. Horner. 1951. Reprint, Oxford: The Pali Text Society, 1996. Volume IV: *Mahāvagga*. Cited as *Vinaya Mahavagga*.

The Book of Discipline (Vinaya-Pitaka). Trans. I. B. Horner. 1952. Reprint, Oxford: The Pali Text Society, 1997. Volume V: *Cullavagga*. Cited as *Vinaya Cullavagga*.

The Book of Gradual Sayings (Anguttara-Nikāya) or More-Numbered Suttas. Trans. E. M. Hare. 1935. Reprint, Oxford: The Pali Text Society, 1995. Volume IV: *The Books of Sevens, Eights and Nines*. Cited as *Anguttara-Nikāya*.

Brower, Michael, and Warren Leon. *The Consumer's Guide to Effective Environmental Choices: Practical Advice from the Union of Concerned Scientists*. New York: Random House, Three Rivers Press, 1999.

Buddhaghosa, Bhadantācariya. *The Path of Purification: Visuddhimagga*. Translated by Bhikkhu Ñāṇamoli. Seattle: Buddhist Publication Society, 1991. Cited as *Visuddhimagga*.

Chodron, Pema. *Start Where You Are: A Guide to Compassionate Living*. Boston: Shambhala Press, 1994.

Cicuzza, Claudio. "The Spiritual Teacher in Theravada Buddhism: Inner Motivations and Foundations for Mindfulness." In *Guru. The Spiritual Master in Eastern and Western Tradition: Authority and Charisma*, ed. Antonio Rigopoulos. Venice, 2004.

The Connected Discourses of the Buddha: A Translation of the Samyutta Nikaya. Trans. Bhikkhu Bodhi. Somerville, MA: Wisdom Publications, 2000. Cited as *Samyutta Nikaya*.

Davis, Stephen F. "Little Pictures in the Mind? Everything You Need to Know about Imagery." PsycCritiques. 49 (Supplement 8) (2004) [np].

Dement, William C. *The Promise of Sleep*. New York: Dell, 1999.

The Dhammapada. Translated by John Ross Carter and Mahinda Palihawadana. Oxford: Oxford University Press, 1987.

Drake, Susan M. "Guided Imagery and Education: Theory, Practice and Experience." *Journal of Mental Imagery*. 18 (1 & 2) (1996): 94–132.

Edmundsen, Mark. *Why Read?* New York: Bloomsbury, 2004.

Eliade, Mircea. *The Sacred and the Profane: The Nature of Religion*. Trans. Willard R. Trask. New York: Harcourt Brace and Company, 1959.

Filene, Peter. *The Joy of Teaching: A Practical Guide for New Teachers*. Chapel Hill, NC: University of North Carolina Press, 2005.

Fink, L. Dee. *Creating Significant Learning Experiences: An Integrated Approach to Designing College Courses*. San Francisco: Jossey-Bass, 2003.

Goldberg, Natalie. *Wild Mind: Living the Writer's Life*. New York: Bantam, 1990.

Goldstein, Joseph. *Insight Meditation: The Practice of Freedom*. Boston: Shambhala Press, 1994.

Gottlieb, Roger. *A Spirituality of Resistance: Finding a Peaceful Heart and Protecting the Earth*. New York: Crossroad Publishing Company, 1999.

Harvey, Peter. *An Introduction to Buddhism*. Cambridge: Cambridge University Press, 1990.

Hendrix, Harville. *Getting the Love You Want: A Guide for Couples*. New York: HarperCollins, 1998.

Heilbrun, Carolyn G. *The Last Gift of Time: Life Beyond Sixty*. New York: The Dial Press, 1997.

Highet, Gilbert. *The Art of Teaching*. New York: Alfred A. Knopf, 1950.

Imagery in Psychology: A Reference Guide. Westport, CT: Praeger, 2004.

Keating, Thomas. *Invitation to Love: The Way of Christian Contemplation*. Continuum International Publishing Group, 1994.

———. *Open Mind, Open Heart: The Contemplative Dimension of the Gospel*. Continuum International Publishing Group, 1994.

Johnson-Bennet, Pam. *Cat vs. Cat: Keeping Peace When You Have More Than One Cat*. New York: Penguin Books, 2004.

Kegan, Robert. *In Over Our Heads: The Mental Demands of Modern Life*. Boston: Harvard University Press, 1994.

Lozanov, Georgi. *Suggestology and Outlines of Suggestopedy*. Translated by Marjorie Hall-Pozharlieva and Krassimira Pashmakova. New York: Gordon and Breach, 1978.

The Long Discourses of the Buddha: A Translation of the Dīgha Nikāya. Trans. Maurice Walsh. Somerville, MA: Wisdom Publications, 1987, 1995. Cited as *Dīgha Nikāya*.

Makransky, John. *Awakening Through Love: Unveiling Your Deepest Goodness*. Boston: Wisdom Publications, 2007.

Macy, Joanna. *Mutual Causality in Buddhism and General Systems Theory: The Dharma of Natural Systems*. Albany, NY: State University of New York Press, 1991.

Macy, Joanna and Molly Young Brown. *Coming Back to Life: Practices to Reconnect Our Lives, Our World*. Gabriola Island, Canada: New Society Publishers, 1998.

McKeachie, Wilbert J. *Teaching Tips: Strategies, Research, and Theory for College and University Teachers*. New York: Houghton Mifflin Company, 1999.

The Middle Length Discourses of the Buddha: A New Translation of the Majjhima Nikāya. Trans. Bhikkhu Bodhi. Somerville, MA: Wisdom Publications, 1995. Cited as *Majjhima Nikāya*.

Ñāṇamoli, Bhikkhu. *The Life of the Buddha: According to the Pali Canon*. Sri Lanka: Buddhist Publication Society, 1972.

Nelson, Craig. "Tools for Tampering with Teaching's Taboos." *New Paradigms for College Teaching*. Edina, MN: Interaction Book Co., 1997.

O'Flaherty, Wendy Doniger. *Women, Androgynes, and Other Mythical Beasts*. Chicago: University of Chicago Press, 1980.

O'Reilly, Mary Rose. *The Peaceable Classroom*. Portsmouth, NH: Boynton/Cook Publishers, 1993.

Orsi, Robert A. *Between Heaven and Earth: The Religious Worlds People Make and the Scholars Who Study Them*. Princeton, NJ: Princeton University Press, 2005.

Palmer, Parker. *The Courage to Teach: Exploring the Inner Landscape of a Teacher's Life*. San Francisco: Jossey-Bass, 1998.

Parkum, Virginia Cohn, and J. Anthony Stultz. "The Angulimala Lineage: Buddhist Prison Ministries." In *Engaged Buddhism in the West*, ed. Christopher S. Queen. Boston: Wisdom Publications, 2000.

Perry, William G., Jr. *Forms of Ethical and Intellectual Development in the College Years: A Scheme*. San Francisco: Jossey-Bass, 1999.

Rahula, Walpola. *What the Buddha Taught*. New York: Grove Press, 1959.

Ratey, John J. *The User's Guide to the Brain: Perception, Attention, and the Four Theaters of the Brain*. New York: Random House, 2001.

Rosenberg, Marshall B. *Nonviolent Communication: A Language of Life*. Encinitas, CA: PuddleDancer Press, 2003.

Salzberg, Sharon. *Loving-kindness: The Revolutionary Art of Happiness*. Boston: Shambhala Press, 1997.

Schacter, Daniel L. *The Seven Sins of Memory: How the Mind Forgets and Remembers*. Boston: Houghton Mifflin, 2001.

Schwartz, Jeffrey M., and Sharon Begley. *The Mind and the Brain: Neuroplasticity and the Power of Mental Force*. New York: HarperCollins, 2002.

Sedgwick, Eve Kosofsky. *Touching Feeling: Affect, Pedagogy, Performativity*. Durham, NC: Duke University Press, 2003.

Shaw, Miranda. *Passionate Enlightenment: Women in Tantric Buddhism*. Princeton, NJ: Princeton University Press, 1994.

Springer, Sally P. *Left Brain, Right Brain: Perspectives from Cognitive Neuroscience*. 5th ed. New York: Freeman, 1998.

Suzuki, Shunryu. *Zen Mind, Beginner's Mind: Informal talks on Zen Meditation and Practice*. New York: Weatherhill, 1970.

Thera, Nyanaponika and Hellmuch Hecker. *Great Disciples of the Buddha: Their Lives, Their Works, Their Legacy*. Boston: Wisdom Publications, 1997.

Wheeler, Kate. Editor's Preface to Pandita, Sayadaw U. The *State of Mind Called Beautiful*. Somerville, MA: Wisdom Publications, 2006.

Williams, Linda Verlee. *Teaching for the Two-Sided Mind: A Guide to Right Brain/ Left Brain Education*. New York: Simon and Schuster, 1983.

Winnicott, D.W. "Playing: Its Theoretical Status in the Clinical Situation" in *The International Journal of Psycho-Analysis* 49 (1968): 591–99.

Yun, Hsing. *Being Good: Buddhist Ethics for Everyday Life*. New York: Weatherhill, 1998.

Index